SILENT TEARS

*Judy,
I hope you find this to be a blessing.
Joshua 1:9
Selma Strudwick*

SILENT TEARS

Selma J. Stroebel

Copyright © 2016 Selma J. Stroebel
All rights reserved.

ISBN-13: 9781534957428
ISBN-10: 1534957421
Library of Congress Control Number: 2016910603
CreateSpace Independent Publishing Platform
North Charleston, South Carolina

1---Genre---Memoir---Non-fiction

2---Author's Bio

The author, Selma Stroebel, grew up in the foothills of western Alberta, Canada, living on a sheep and cattle ranch during her very early years of life. Many hours and days were spent herding sheep, helping with cattle drives, involving herself with harvesting, and other ranch duties. But as fate would have it that lifestyle became intermittent due to family circumstances. In order to get her primary education she had to live with other families, one who didn't speak English. Her high school experience involved leaving home full time and going to a boarding school where she met students from around the globe. Moving to Milwaukee, Wisconsin with her native born and Harvard educated husband where they lived for many years, raising and traveling with their children. Later she studied interior design at Madison Area Technical College in Wisconsin after which she did freelance work. Currently she and her husband spend their summers in the Wisconsin Dells area of central Wisconsin living in the home they built with their own hands. Winters are spent in warm sunny California close to Palm Springs where they enjoy camping and ATV adventures. Time spent with their children and five grandchildren are a top priority.

Cover Photo: This photo is of the author as a young girl on her parent's ranch.

3----

This is a memoir of a young girl growing up in the shadow of a deep family mystery which profoundly affected the author throughout her life.

Having the seeming advantage of living on a cattle and sheep ranch would appear like an idealistic lifestyle. However, the author found herself at a young age suffering from deep depression with no knowledge or help for a pathway out of her condition.

Significant events began to change the direction of her life but mysteries regarding her family were so shadowy that any understanding proved impossible. While continuously puzzled by her father's mysterious behavior and watching her talented, intelligent, hardworking mother be confronted with false accusations, wounded the young girl deeply.

Meanwhile the positive influence of her trail-blazing, adventurous grandfather and capable stylish grandmother provided a stabilizing alternative to her fractured home life.

Recovery from her own depression and her search to become a strong, independent woman within the adventurous life of her husband and three children, she reached out to her faith. She found strength for the days and eventual peace amidst the journey.

A haunting force drove her for decades to uncover the obscure reasons for her father's unusual irrational behavior and all its ramifications for her life. Little by little revelations came. Read her story to find out how she found the answers and an eventual lasting peace with the forces that shaped her life.

Dedications

Dedication of this memoir is to the legacy of the life my mother lived. Her belief and faith in a loving Heavenly Father who has promised to provide and guide during times of extreme challenges were her guideposts. Disappointments which seem overwhelming and impossible to overcome can destroy hope but Mother never gave into those feelings. During her era a woman managing a male dominated business in a man's world was not a common practice. Instead, out of necessity she blazed her own trail with amazing success. Her talents went unrecognized by others as she so purposely strived to fulfill the calling of providing for her family in a masculine dominated society. Her talents and intelligence became much more apparent after taking the time to review the era in which she lived and the mountainous obstacles which she faced.

Her faith, perseverance through much difficulty, her obvious intelligence, and business acuity, has provided an example of a life lived with purpose and dignity. Most would have folded up their tent and sought a much easier path or even a dependant one at the expense of the taxpayer. An easy path was not in mother's mindset. Quitting was not her style.

Appreciations

Conflict whirled around in my mind regarding the writing of a memoir. As I shared life experiences and stories of the past a common comment was: "You should write a book." Brain seeds were being planted as a result of those comments. In time those seeds began to take root.

Presenting the first rough drafts of my writings to friends came the responses of: "Keep going, don't quit." I took them at their word as that was helping to build my confidence and purpose for continuing with my project. Inner conflict had caused me to second guess myself, a hound that kept nipping at my heels. As I continued to write, those self doubting thoughts kept fading and a compelling purpose emerged. True friends see things in us that we don't see in ourselves.

Without the encouragement of my dear friends this project would probably be laying in a closed notebook somewhere. Sandy Reiter and Betty Heller Hobbs were two that encouraged me to not give up but to keep going. "You have a story to tell" were their comments. My dear friend Kathryn Quillin spent many hours editing and checking every detail. Until she presented herself with her editing services I was wandering in a writer's wilderness. Without her input the notebook form would be the final draft. Susan Winstead was very encouraging to me in pointing out the broad scope of everyday life experiences which were great in describing strong women and how they defied the odds. Katherine Hughes spent time reading and checking for thought connections and transitions. Daughter, Karen Taylor, made herself available with her much needed input. The contributions made to my project by these ladies are invaluable.

Extending much appreciation to friends who have given generously for time contributed to reading my rough drafts, encouragement freely given, and lending their listening ears to someone who likes to keep repeating herself.

Contents

Dedications · vii
Appreciations · ix
Introduction · xiii

Fish Bowl Life · 1
Transitions · 10
Summer Trips · 22
Significance Almost Missed · 54
Sacred Moments · 58
Promises of a New World · 62
Heading North to Alberta · 68
Life on the Homestead · 73
A New Direction · 82
Garfield Samuel Thompson · 90
Father of Lock Leven Trout · 96
Nanny Edna Thompson-- Nee--Abshire · · · · · · · · · · · · · · · · · · 101
Grandpa Garfield and Grandma Nanny's Home site · · · · · · · · · · · 112
Living Life in the River Valley · 116
Establishing Life in the River Valley · 149
Getting an Education · 160
Establishing My Own Faith · 176
Virginia Edna Fletcher-- Nee--Thompson · · · · · · · · · · · · · · · · · 178
Frances Arthur Dennis Fletcher · 195

Berry Picking · 207
Social Life in the River Valley · · · · · · · · · · · · · · · · · · · 216
Piecing Together a Puzzle · 224
Peace Finally Comes · 235

On Hallowed Ground · 243

Introduction

EARLY MORNING FOG

MY LIFE'S PERSONAL PHILOSOPHY has come about through personal trials, an inquiring mind, and quiet contemplation which I love. I love the silence of the moment, letting my mind wander off into the green pastures of fantasy or into the shadows of reality. Recalling sweet memories is like taking a mini vacation. Recalling stresses, turmoil, and strife in one's life can be like a personal war of dueling forces exploding to disturb the cherished moments of peace that can come too seldom.

I love to sit in the rocker that came from my mother's parent's old farm house. That rocker is a special place for me. I can see my grandfather sitting in it, whittling his wooden creations with his ever present pocket knife. One of his favorite things to whittle was his wooden eggs. These eggs were placed in the hen's nests to attract them to the appropriate location to lay their eggs.

I somehow feel close to Grandpa while sitting there. I can hear his gravelly voice, see his withering body, and smell the scent of wood smoke that has permeated the fibers of his clothing. This was his daily cologne. Their simple country life-style had become a way of life they were content with.

Selma J. Stroebel

Finding the time to share a few moments with my favorite piece of furniture, in a quiet state of mind, comes too seldom. These are meaningful moments for me. It is during these rest breaks that insights to life come, bringing solace to the spirit and peace of mind. Sitting in this rocker which has long been removed from its original scene, stirs my memories of events that are long gone. Sitting in this rocker viewing scenes of nature through my sunroom window, taking in the beauty of nature, recalling memories of good along with the difficult, reminds me of how life has changed and how much more I now understand.

Contemplation time is my time. It's for me and not a time to give to others. Trying to shut out what I need to be doing in that moment, rather than sitting in that rocker, takes some denial of responsibilities. I need some dream time. It's the time I can dream my dreams, fantasize and visualize the improbable or seemingly the impossible. Then sometimes the seemingly impossible gives birth to an open door of possibility. Creative juices begin to flow again and life suddenly has renewed meaning. Life begins to become more meaningful and less hectic. Being able to discard the cloak of urgency enables my inner spirit to be renewed again.

The stirring of memories that are long gone cause the world of materialism to fade away, like an early morning fog that dissipates with the rising of an early morning sun sharing its light with all of life.

This time spent alone with myself helps me to be conscious of the fact that I am happy being me. This is a complete reversal of my personal history. I am comfortable with who I am. The interests that I have cultivated, the education which I have attained, the personal relationships whether family or friends that have crossed my life's path, all have enriched my life beyond measure.

Actually, I'm surprised at myself, as I have not always been this way. I am surprised at this gift of tranquility. I have to ask myself where did this come from? Then I remember it in its truer form. The journey of life and its lessons learned.

Silent Tears

Traveling through life is a trip that cannot be compared with another. Experiences that are of the great challenge nature are always personal and unique, but at the same time common to all. Similarities exist to all humanity but the personal is always special to each of us. Everyone has a story of their own.

Personal trials have many sources. Some of them come to us from our own doing. Others may be from the effect of what someone else has done. We can experience consequences in our lives that can have either short-term or long-term results. Neuroses and failures can be part of our life's picture. Successes can be elusive. Without outside help or sound instruction from sources like parents, grandparents, schools, churches, etc., we were born into this world, placed into the care of adults that surround us without us having any influence to choose the level of care we would receive. If the care we received was a healthy functional one or of an unhealthy dysfunctional type is a reminder that everyone born lives with different levels of functionality. We must remember that we are all human where no perfection exists. Remember the Biblical first family. Cain became jealous of his brother, Abel, and murdered him. The human condition of dysfunction started more than a generation ago. It has been around for very a long time. That is why this world needs a savior. God has provided an answer to our broken condition through His Son, Jesus, as told to us through the Christmas and Easter stories. We can discover this treasure by taking the time to internalize the truth of God's gift as we celebrate these traditions.

Beyond the psychological side of life there are times when health problems arise. At birth sometimes disabilities present themselves through no fault of the one being affected. Reality is that all of us are born with genetic tendencies toward some ailment or weakness. No matter how much we want to avoid the thought, a day or moment will come that will be beyond our ability to control all the events of our lives.

Selma J. Stroebel

Unanswered questions have a way of nipping at our heels. We can become driven by fear or anxiety. Our inner spirit can become restless and possibly aimless. Anger and resentments helping to create some of life's dysfunctions can raise their ugly heads crippling our inner life force. We can react to life itself in a very negative way, suffocating any possible joy we could have. Depression can become a constant companion. Despair, loss of hope, and the feeling that life is not worth living, can become a hat that is worn daily. I know all about this as this was the life I lived for many years. Too often, suicide is the end result instead of love, joy, peace and contentment. Jesus said "I came that you may have life and have it more abundantly", John 10:10, which is a promise from Him that seems unattainable.

Today I am happy, healthy, and still dreaming, even though I am in the autumn years of my life. How did I grow out of my depression into a healthy state of mind? How have I discovered fullness of life in spite of the valleys and trenches along the way? What kind of legacy do I want to leave my family?

I now have a healthy workable philosophy that has been fulfilling. Positive thoughts fill my mind when I am feasting my eyes on my favorite painting, or viewing a special scene in nature, realizing that nothing happens by accident. All is part of a much greater plan than man could never conceive. Yes, we are the sum total of our experiences, but also a lot more. "No eye has seen, no ear has heard, no mind has conceived what God has prepared for those who love Him." I Corinthians 2:9.

I now relax and enjoy my time, in my restored grandfather's rocker. However, in the distance of my mind like a far away mirage, I see something, but I don't want to recognize what that might be. There is a distant rumble which echoes louder and louder disturbing my serenity. I can't seem to quiet this disturbance which continues to cause a restlessness in my inner soul. I feel this restlessness evolving into a passion that is haunting me to the point that I can no longer ignore it. Since I have had lots of practice tuning out those things which I prefer not to think about ---I do just that ---for a time.

Even though I had come to the point in my life that I was happy being me, and very much at peace with myself, my ability to absorb some important realities were blocked nor was I fully conscious of them. The landscape of my mind had become cluttered and deadened with past frustrations. Responsibilities, raising my own family, mundane daily routine of life, along with our present family dysfunctions, had been a buffer helping me to avoid the past. However, restlessness remained at the core of my being.

Where does this restlessness come from, I ask myself? Why does it keep re-occurring? Is there something more I need to accomplish before life has reached its conclusion? Is there a higher meaning to all of this? If so, what is it? Why have I felt so conflicted? Hasn't God agreed to direct my path, as I recall a scriptural promise? These thoughts and questions keep on dogging me.

Direction setting moments can go by unnoticed like the last dirty shirt thrown to the laundry basket, or lost like a floating feather carried by the wind setting itself into a weed patch. These moments can become lost forever unless something grabs our attention causing us to take note. Significant moments rarely march into the rooms of our lives shouting or waving a flag to catch our attention. Sometimes there might just be a whisper of a thought that says to us; take note. I have learned that whispers are one of God's methods of communication with His children.

Resistance had danced around in my head, tap dancing like a fairy on the head of a pin. However, a spiritual dimension was starting to evolve in my mind. This dimension was growing into a much bigger and broader picture, a vision that seemed overwhelming. I recalled a simple and routine scene from the past that had seared itself into my consciousness. From time to time I had recalled this scene trying to absorb all that it meant, but had let it's reality slip into the distance of time. I had been letting it fade away with all of its significance unless I determined to record it.

Was the fog lifting in my mind? I finally realized that I needed to become serious about preserving what is easily lost. More questions disturbed my thinking with no clear direction. How in the world am I going to develop this? Where do I begin? What are my real purposes in writing a memoir?

As I have considered those questions and the last one in particular, some goals evolved which I felt had to be met. The passion for continuing did not let up but kept intensifying.

The requirements and goals I have set for myself have to include the following:

1) A tribute to my mother, who was hero like none other
2) That my family would know their history and heritage
3) That my family would learn of their ancestor's spiritual legacy
4) That life does not have to be lived in the spirit of defeat
5) Hope for a personal legacy that demonstrates a listening ear for God's leadership and an eye that recognizes His truth.

Fish Bowl Life

September---1957

MY HUSBAND Jim and I met at Canadian Nazarene College, in Red Deer, Alberta, Canada, where he was on staff and I was a student. Our dating time was a case of student dates professor.

Jim was a mathematics, science, physics, and physical education teacher in the high school department of this private school. He loved to experiment with chemicals and challenge his students, all of which provided an outlet for his fun craving and creative personality. He had gained the reputation of having regular explosions in his lab as it was not unusual for smoke to be rolling out from under his lab room door. Not having a quiet type of personality, drama in and around his lab was a common occurrence.

In spite of all the uproar he could create, he loved the academic challenge of working with the exceptional learning curve of bright students. His job was to prepare his students for the provincial departmental exams that each student had to take at the end of the school year. These exams were prepared by the provincial government, not by the local school district or by the current instructor of that course. These were challenging tests to prepare for. The student's test scores would determine whether they would be eligible to attend university or not. These were eliminator tests, so preparation had to be taken very seriously. With motivated students he thoroughly enjoyed this employment opportunity, exposing the truly talented person that he was.

Selma J. Stroebel

Jim had grown up in Milwaukee, Wisconsin, immigrating to Canada to work as an educational instructor, learning about this opportunity through the private university he had just graduated from.

The idea of leaving the USA for an adventure and the experience of another country was a natural draw to his adventurous spirit. After spending a year at a central Illinois private college along with his three intense years at Harvard University, leaving the country for this totally new experience seemed like an opportunity which he could not turn down. Thus, loading his small inventory of possessions into his 1953 Ford hardtop, another phase of his life was birthed.

One year after Jim had been on staff, I enrolled in the college department with no clear set goals in mind for myself. Emotionally, I was trying my best to hold my life together. I was having difficulty functioning in any normal fashion. My memory and my ability to concentrate were functioning at a greatly reduced level which was also affecting my academic progress. I knew I needed help. I would have loved to have had some counseling but that kind of help did not exist at that time nor could I have afforded it if available. Psychological counseling was not something that was in societies' vocabulary. When it did become acknowledged as a field, much resistance was verbalized especially by some groups.

I badly needed a new beginning. Caught in a dark tunnel of hopelessness with no thought in sight of ever being successful was draining my life blood of energy. Friends that I had gone to school with, now had become professionals with admirable careers making me feel more hopeless and inferior. Their successes definitively were not helping me feel better about myself and were beyond my reach in my current state of mind. I was spiraling down into a pond of despair getting stuck in the mud at the bottom with no snorkel to provide air for survival. With no life raft to grab, I had come to the conclusion that life was not worth living. Understanding how I had spiraled into this condition was a dark cloud of mixed emotions with no answers. I only knew that our family life was dysfunctional and this dark cloud of hopelessness hung over our lives.

Silent Tears

I was hoping that leaving home and going away to college would help me find a new beginning, maybe even find a way to gain a better outlook on life. I did not know what kind of path to pursue to accomplish that. In my dim view of life, emotional stability and personal peace was maybe a possibility. With no solutions in mind, I felt the need to pray. I asked God to heal my mind. Since I didn't like the way I was feeling or the person I had become, it was a prayer that came to me out of the blue. That prayer was not premeditated but only a fleeting thought. It didn't seem to be a solution but only a thought that drifted through my mind at the moment but is an act that has remained in my memory. My inner turmoil had so consumed me that my ability to express any kind of emotion had totally flat-lined. I earnestly felt the need to hide my inner conflict. I didn't want anyone to know how distorted I felt. Normal, in my mind, was that which was modeled by others who seemed to be successful, but in my current state of mind, unattainable.

I started the fall semester by signing up for some general classes, along with a book-keeping course. I felt those kind of classes would be manageable. That filled my schedule as I tried to settle into an academic life routine, constantly trying and desperately needing to hide my inner emotional war. At the same time I was hoping for a path out of my despair.

I was now getting to know my roommate. Our growing up environs were rather different. She was from the southern prairie land of Alberta while I had experienced the foothills and the Rockies of the western region.

Living in a dormitory can have its challenges, but as it turned out we were quite compatible. We both liked a neat room with our clothes hung up, no clutter on the floor, and our beds made every morning as well. We could even agree on the temperature of the thermostat and also when to open and close our dorm room window. Sounds boring, but it was a friendly arrangement. Ours was better than some which we heard about.

Every school seems to have their own tradition and one which existed at this private school was a get acquainted party at the end of the first month. All the students and faculty customarily attended.

My roommate wanted me to go with her. I hesitated, but decided that it would be good for me to go. Clinging to my social avoidance and the need for solitude, through my roommate's insistence the idea of a party prevailed. I didn't have a party dress, however, I was able to borrow one from my sister-in-law. Fortunately, my brother and his wife lived locally so she quickly volunteered her dark rose pink velour dress as I told her about the upcoming occasion.

That Friday night was the beginning of a huge change. He was of medium height with very dark hair and a mustache. I don't remember the first words we exchanged but I remember his powerful presence.

After that get acquainted party students began to notice the time we would spend together. It didn't take long for them to start making their teasing comments which became a constant. With Jim and his gregarious personality, he was loving every minute of it while I just wanted to be left alone going unnoticed about my student life. Being thrust into such prominence of academic life was something I was totally unprepared for. Obviously, being left alone was something that was not going to happen.

Expectations of me were beginning to change as I was expected to become a leader for events. I was asked to be a reporter for the school newspaper which definitely was not my calling. Trying to keep a low profile, staying out of the limelight, and communicate signals that I was not at all interested in this fish bowl life, just added another dimension to my emotional battle.

As the school year progressed, I learned that some of the female staff members were jealous of me. One approached me and told me so in her personally chosen words. Obviously they were hoping to be the ones who dated Jim instead of it being me.

Silent Tears

Jim was loving all of this attention and was thriving on it. Since I was never into the habit of talking about myself, I was beginning to feel that I was at least being able to hide my depression.

We had now been dating for a number of months, and I was thinking it was now time to introduce Jim to my family. I took him to my grandparents' place first as their house was much more presentable. My home conditions would not have given a very good impression and was something I dreaded, as I was embarrassed to introduce him to our farm life.

In time I realized that our family situation was very complex and was much more involved than what seemed obvious. I had lived so close to these problems that my ability to cope and understand was extremely limited, living with a fog-like mind set. Needles to say, I was not able to do much explaining to Jim. Meeting my parents didn't seem to scare him off. Later, he told me he recognized some of my families' problems but was impressed with my mother's intelligence. First impressions hadn't bothered him. In time, both he and I progressed in our actual understanding of the depth and complexity that existed, however, it took a lot longer than my mind ever conceived.

Our relationship was leading to that proposal question, I could tell. I needed some direction in my thinking. I was feeling very comfortable with Jim and was very impressed with his intelligence.

I have learned that God winks or whispers come in unusual and unexpected ways. Three times God sent whispers my direction within a twenty four hour period.

The first whisper came through a conversation which I was having with the Dean of the school. At some point in our conversation he encouraged me by saying, "All things work together for good to them who love God and are called according to His purpose." I listened and thought about our conversation.

Next morning, came whisper number two. Morning chapel is a requirement for all students to attend before classes begin. The preliminaries had all taken place, the speaker stood to speak and his first words were "All things work together for good to them who love God and are called according to His purpose." This was his driving point for the current presentation. This got my attention as I recalled the prior conversation from the previous day. Chapel being over, we all headed for the business of the day. This sure is a coincidence, I thought, but put it out of my mind as there were other things to think about.

Student life has a routine all of its own in preparation for a day filled with academic stimulus. Trying to rise and shine with a smile, clean your room, make your bed, hang up your clothes, and be ready for room inspection at any time. Then take some time for reading and meditation, and head for the dining hall for some physical nourishment.

During my meditation time, there were those words again as my eyes glanced over my intended morning reading. Romans 8:28 "All things work together for good to them who love God and are called according to His purpose". These words were no longer a coincidence but a Divine direction which I felt had some definite meaning for me. I felt I had just experienced another God whisper in my life, nudging me to take note, as He had some specific plans.

My concentration problem was slightly improving but my memory was requiring major effort. I recall sitting in the school library trying to study when my mind drifted off to my home life. While trying to visualize the physical images of my home, the images would not come. I could not visualize our house. I tried to bring forward into my mind my home's images but nothing came to me. They would not return to my consciousness. I had seemingly blanked out. Needless to say, I sat there in shock. I realized then how close I had come to a total breakdown. It was scary to think that one could lose such a vital part of their mind. I realized the stress I had been living under had really taken its toll. My path out of this condition remained an unknown, adding another layer of stress. Knowing that you are living a life of emotional instability corrodes your innermost sense of self. After processing these thoughts, my mind came back to the present, helping me diffuse those shaken moments which were reminding me of the emotional state I was still in and how bad off I had really become.

Planning for our wedding was another stress maker along with this fishbowl life. What should have been a happy year instead was one that was shadowy and difficult with the ongoing fog of trying to hold my life together. I was still trying to keep my condition completely to myself, feeling it would be way too risky to reveal any of my tumultuous emotions to anyone.

Wedding plans came together little by little with some help from my sister-in-law who was basically my only help. My fear was that I would not be able to plan a respectable event that would reflect the career my husband to be possessed. I had not attended weddings prior to our own so a fear of missing some real important details or making a choice of poor taste bothered me greatly. Money was in short supply as well.

Jim and I were both conservative in the money department. We conserved in whatever way we could. Jim's wool suit came from a thrift store and I shopped for the cheapest most acceptable wedding dress that I could find. Our wedding rings were simple gold bands. We were both used to conserving so we were in full agreement regarding money matters.

Our reception was also simple. We served Mother's home canned chicken and canned peaches along with some dinner rolls. Our wedding cake was English style, meaning that the tiered layers were a fruit cake topped with hard candied icing. The custom was to save the top tier, preserve it until your seventh anniversary, then partake and share. However, we did not wait that long as we moved out of the country one year later.

We were married nine months after we met. Our guests were school staff, some of Jim's students, and my family. Jim's family was unable to travel from Wisconsin at that time.

We had a church candlelight service with my brother walking me down the aisle. There was no way I was going to have my father walk with me as I had no confidence in him for anything. Nor did I want to be identified with him.

My state of mind had kept me from fully enjoying our dating time, my school year, and all that was involved with the wedding and its preparation. Rather than being happy and excited I was relieved. Relieved that this fish bowl life was over and life could go on in a more normal fashion. I was feeling more alive but I had felt dead and numb for so long, much of that feeling was still with me. It was remaining a constant struggle to overcome. In time, this experience would be helpful in understanding others who struggled with the same dark cloud of depression that hangs over their lives.

Jim planned a beautiful honeymoon trip to the photogenic Banff National Park. We really enjoyed the outdoor activities of hiking, canoeing, horseback riding, and of course, sightseeing the magnificent mountain peaks, valleys and the beautiful Lake Louise. It was hard to leave the majesty of it all and the wonder of God's creation. His artistry of contrasts between the blue green water of Lake Louise, surrounded by mountain peaks, then being kissed with a glacier at the southern end of the Lake, draws your eyes and soul like a magnet.

Other than Jim's movie camera, we didn't carry much other equipment. In our ignorance we set up his movie camera to film some black bears that were nearby. This one bear heard the camera rolling, came over and knocked the tripod right out from underneath sending the whole unit flying through the air. At the same time, a game warden saw this whole act on our part, resulting in a verbal lashing. Endangering ourselves in the presence of these wild animals knowing the park warden was right, we should have known better.

Silent Tears

Two weeks after our wedding, we were separated for the summer. Jim attended the University of Alberta in Edmonton living in a studio apartment for six weeks, while I continued to live in our one bedroom apartment in Red Deer. In the meantime, I got a job working at the Provincial Institute caring for the handicapped and mentally retarded, as they were called then. Today we refer to such patients as the physically and mentally challenged, which is much less demeaning. Families who have these challenges need all the respect and support we can possibly honor them with. These families experience a lot of personal pain and face challenges that are overwhelming. Our adult son and family have had an extremely challenging situation as their middle child has Angelman's Syndrome, a condition resulting from an incomplete chromosome fifteen.

Fall brought much needed routine. We needed time for each other. Jim was back to his teaching position and we were enjoying our one bedroom apartment.

As that school year ended our plans changed. Jim wanted to return to his home state of Wisconsin and back to his home town of Milwaukee. We boxed up everything we owned, hauled it down to the train station, and had it all shipped by rail to Milwaukee. I was dubious about the safety of our belongings since we were not the best of packers. When our belongings arrived in downtown Milwaukee and after unpacking, the only thing which I could determine was missing was my hamburger patty press. Things had gone better than I anticipated after all.

Three weeks after our move to Milwaukee, Wisconsin, our daughter was born, and through contacts which Jim had previously made, a job opening was available at a local high school.

Transitions

I HAD NEVER TRAVELED beyond the borders of Alberta before and moving to Wisconsin was a totally new experience.

Alberta was a dry climate while Wisconsin had a lot of humidity. A slice of bread on the kitchen counter could dry out in an hour in the arid climate, versus taking a week to dry. Humid days in Wisconsin would have water droplets gathering on hand rails with no evidence of rain in the air. You could shower and an hour later you felt like you needed another one. Your perspiration just didn't evaporate making your clothes became irritatingly damp or even unsightly in places which were not attractive or desired. Humidity was something new I was learning to live with.

Milwaukee was a city heavily influenced with continental European traditions and customs while I had grown up with old English influences. Canadians were much less rigid. We served tea in bone china cups and dinner on china plates to workmen who had just come in from a hard day's work. Sometimes linen finery was used but flexibility was always in vogue. Bone china was reasonably priced and readily available then. Milwaukeeans saved their fine china for formal or special occasions with all their finery of linens and crystal on display. Jim's mother informed me that there was a very proper way to use china and anything less than that was very incorrect. Eclectic table settings were definitely not in vogue.

In Milwaukee beer came from the tap, while in Alberta that is where you got your drink of water. In Jim's family, you knew what day of the week it was by their meal menu of the day. Also, after eating your dinner, which was exactly at five-fifteen every day, you were to sit for awhile as an aid to your digestion. In my household, we ate when we got hungry no matter the hour. Also we were lucky if we weren't dealing with some kind of an emergency either during or after the meal. We were always on edge about something. Being flexible was more than a custom, but a necessity. Sitting a spell after you finished eating in our farm environment was an impossible act to practice.

Our edginess was either based on something that had just happened, or something we were afraid of happening. Our farm life was so dysfunctional it challenged your wits. We had lots of problems in our family but rigidity was not one of them. Jim's family rolled their eyes and raised their eyebrows more than once at my free-wheeling spirit. Even feeding the baby her bottle had to be done on the minute. After moving into our own apartment our baby got fed when the kid got hungry. Rigidity was not going to become a new resident in my life.

Moving to Wisconsin and away from family did not unnerve me. Jim and I had each other. I had already experienced so many living changes that it was a normal state of being for me.

Between the time of our arrival in Milwaukee and the birth of our daughter, those three weeks were spent acquainting ourselves with the medical care available to us. I had to adjust to the idea of a new doctor for late stage pregnancy and a hospital that I wasn't familiar with.

We didn't have our own apartment for the first six weeks after our arrival. We were living with Jim's parents. Getting to know his family and their habits was a big change especially adjusting to their ultra organized habits and my open ended figure it out as you go attitude. Our differences were a challenge for all involved. Changes were nothing new to me so I was able to take most of it with an even keel spirit, most of the time.

I learned the skills I had previously used in dealing with difficult people was an education that came in handy while living with his parents. It became apparent that his mother was jealous of me as she was accusing me of being jealous of her when Jim kissed her goodbye when leaving after a visit. It took about an hour for me to figure that one out. I certainly knew I wasn't jealous of her nor could I care less about how goodbyes were exchanged between the two of them. I decided the best solution to this situation was to tell Jim directly that I didn't care, but also that he should kiss his mother goodbye. I didn't want him to feel that he was being caught in the middle. That mattered to me as I knew he would not know how to deal with it. His relationship with his mother was already strained with friction between them that had been going on for a long time. This kind of friction was no stranger to me, but what I really wanted was a solution to stem any further agitation between us and his family.

My personal goal for our relationship with his parents was that Jim could have as healthy a relationship as was possible with them. I did not want to be an interference in that relationship but also would like to know that they respected me. Our children needed to know their grandparents and the heritage they would have through them. I determined that I would never bad mouth my husband's parents to my kids. What they would know of them would be of their own experience. I did not want to color their opinion of their grandparents by my own words and emotions. I determined that I would find a way to get along with them somehow. I did not want to become the issue and be a part of adding any more stress to a scene that already had plenty. I could not control them but I had control over my own reactions.

I have learned when dealing with those who are emotionally needy, imaginations can get carried away visualizing all sorts of scenarios. These scenarios that are imagined can become truth to the mind, birthing all kinds of neuroses. All sorts of hair (unrelated and imagined ideas) can be added to statements, creating falsehoods that are difficult to deal with. That is the situation I found myself unwillingly involved with. When I would innocently make a statement, responding with natural reactions and having absolutely no intention of hurting anyone, I would later find myself receiving my statements back, word for word from Jim's mother. Only now, added to my statements was a lot of hair along with her interpretation of my motives. Some of the accusations I was guilty of in her mind, I couldn't have dreamed up in my wildest imagination.

When this started happening I did get upset. How my mother-in-law was taking the privilege of describing me in these negative terms became extremely bothersome. I had been working on my own attitude toward myself and felt like I had made some improvements but now I was this twenty something dealing with this late forty something. I had always tried to respect those who were older than I and felt that I would receive the same in return. This time that principle was not working. How was I going to deal with this? A short description of her was that of an emotional bully. Sometimes Jim's father would join in with her but seldom. I could not let this continue. Somehow some boundaries had to be set requiring a skill that I had not learned to use. It was obvious to me that his parents did not like me since I was resisting their control.

As I am reviewing these scenes in my mind, the clarity of thinking which I managed to possess in order to deal with my husband's mother comes as a surprise to me. I was a long way from feeling emotionally well at the time. I was still living in my own fog. As I review these scenes in my mind I don't see how I could have dealt with the situation any differently. Boundary setting was not something which I had found an easy practice to perform, especially when dealing with opinionated in-laws. However, I felt that I had no choice. Thinking of a solution took some reflective thinking on my part. Since my husband's relationship with his parents was a strained one I did not want to involve him with my solution. I was afraid of adding fuel to an already existing conflict which might spill over into our relationship.

Selma J. Stroebel

My comments in conversation were becoming fuel for wild conclusions regarding me and any motives which I seemed to possess. It occurred to me that if I didn't say anything I wouldn't be accountable for anything. Thinking about that for a time, I decided that would be my new technique for dealing with this dilemma. I decided that if his mother asked me a question, I would reply with the most non-informational answer as possible, and yet give the appearance of politeness. I would then turn the conversation back to her so that she would have to do the talking. I decided that when I was in her presence I would not talk beyond any niceties. As I practiced this technique I discovered that this method worked very well. If it was at all possible I was not going to provide any more fuel for her fire.

I had a strong desire for Jim and our children to have a good relationship with his parents. Any sacrifice I needed to make would be worth it. My own past experience in the area of family relations had provided some insights which gave me warning signals of negative attitudes. More family conflict was something I deeply wanted to avoid. I did not want to be a part of causing any friction within my husband's family, however, I would become a negative focus for his mother no matter how much I tried to avoid her acidity. Each get-together presented new challenges that called for new solutions. We managed to get together for special occasions with some civility being able to build some family memories. To me that spelled success.

My mother in law never did get beyond her jealousy. However, I was very fortunate as my husband always supported me. After her passing away, he informed me she thought I was a terrible mother, abusive to him, as well as a litany of other things she managed to include with her list. I appreciate the fact he never mentioned her opinions while she was living. I probably would not have given her the respect I felt I owed. Our relationship could have turned really ugly.

During my first encounters with Jim's mother, I felt very intimidated. She was a very artistic and talented woman in many ways. Through

Silent Tears

her sewing projects, she designed some beautiful garments for herself, whether it was something simple or something that involved detailed tailoring. She did beautiful needlework that was outstanding, giving to family members as gifts on special occasions. Her goal was perfection in everything she did. These characteristics revealed themselves in a very evident manner during a quilting project. This queen sized quilt was assembled on a fine threaded ecru colored muslin fabric, which she had searched specifically for this project. She created her own designs on this special fabric, using a tone on tone method. She used a variety of stitches but many were French Knots. Some stitches which she used were specifically created by her. The finished product was an outstanding piece of work, leaving no doubt in one's mind about her perfectionist drive and her artistic ability.

His mother was a very hard working woman who worked long hours in their dry cleaning business. She had also developed a very good memory. She claimed that her memory was photographic which perhaps it was. I just know that statements I made came back to me word for word with her own interpretations added. Needless to say, her version of my motives and my version were quite different. Whenever I was in her presence, I was always on the defensive wondering how I was going to survive this visit. Our gatherings were a challenge of the mind to cope with her accusations. Every visit had a different issue and always a surprise as to what the subject would be.

When I internalized all that was happening and gave this situation a lot of thought this led me to my non-talking technique. This method gave me a chance to consider some of the observations which I was making. I had not as of yet articulated these to myself. I had allowed myself to be intimidated by her as she was my elder with life experiences which I had not had. Being in her presence was unnerving.

My non-talking technique began to pay off. It gave me the silence of mind which I needed to really listen to her. I began to absorb some realities regarding this very unhappy, insecure woman who had an inferiority complex. These attributes were dominating her psychologically and had been a long-term internal struggle in her life.

Everyone has a story. Little by little it was revealed to me her own story of trauma and deprivation that she had experienced as a child growing up. She was the youngest of six children, being only four years old when her father passed. This left her mother to raise these children all on her own. Opportunities of employment for women were very limited. Even skilled workers were mostly limited to nursing or teaching positions. The economy and society was not friendly to any woman working in any kind of employment, other than house cleaning or doing someone else's laundry.

As a family they really struggled to survive, just to have food to eat, clothes to wear, along with a roof over their heads. Her family had had it tough. Due to all of the distress in her life, I began to understand how the lack of early nurturing had affected her emotionally to the depth which it had.

Her story, shared by bits and pieces, which came to light over a period of time, revealed a family's true struggle not only for the material side of life but the largest deprivation was the lack of emotional support and development. Emotional deprivation had been a huge factor in her family's struggle for survival.

Gaining insights into my husband's mother, translated into a much better understanding of the person both Jim and I were dealing with. Over time it allowed me to let go of my resentments being able to exchange them for sympathy and empathy.

Leaving my familiar but stressed life in Alberta, to a new one in Wisconsin was a transition in geography but the biggest transition was from my old life of depression to a new life of better mental health. However, morphing fully from one to the other had spanned a lot of years. Practicing new thought patterns, learning to recognize the symptoms of unhealthy thinking, and the continued pursuit of better mental health was always present. This process began with a pivotal event.

Jim was experiencing dental problems and there seemed to be no answer. After visiting several dentists and due to a lot of extreme dental discomfort, he reached the point that he couldn't go on. The pain had become unbearable. After several appointments the dentists could find no reason for his pain. Both he and I had reached our wits end regarding this ongoing seemingly unsolvable oral condition.

One mid-afternoon he came home from work informing me that he could no longer endure the pain as it had reached an intolerable level. We had run out of known options. I recalled some information which I had become aware of a couple of weeks prior. That info involved a clinic located in another town about an hour and a half away from Milwaukee. This clinic had diagnosed a physical ailment for my friend's mother. My friend had kept running into dead ends with no solutions offered at other medical centers. I decided to give this clinic a call.

Pressing the issue of this emergency, I was able to get an appointment quickly for Jim the following day with an ears, nose, and throat specialist. Out of that appointment came the need for a Caldwell operation. Jim had so much sinus scar tissue the doctor claimed it could not be ignored in case there was a cancer present. Sinus infections were something which Jim had experienced a lot of.

Recovery from the surgery seemed to be progressing normally except for a lot of continuing pain. When Jim was to return for his second check up, I informed him that I was going to talk to his doctor before he went in. I felt this remaining pain was abnormal and lasting much longer than it should have. I wanted the doctor to know of my concerns. This doctor was a good listener allowing us to have an in-depth conversation. Through his prior sessions with my husband he related some aspects of Jim's outlook on life that were not healthy. He also shared that there should be no lingering pain but felt that Jim was worrying about life in an unhealthy way and that was affecting him physically.

Jim had already been a help to me and my own mental health issues through refocusing from my former life to the present one. However, I also realized that we both had melancholy personalities and that was not helping either of us emotionally. We were having many good times but also were looking at life through very dim glasses. His doctor helped me to see that fact much more clearly.

During the time Jim was having his medical appointment I sat in the waiting room thinking over the thoughts that his doctor and I had discussed. Sitting and waiting for Jim to return, I made a conscious decision. Whenever Jim made a negative statement, even though there was always some truth connected to his point of view, I determined that I was going to take the opposite position; debate form. I felt the need to confront this negativity which we were bestowing onto ourselves. Negativity was affecting us both and this needed to change. I was going to have to instigate this new way of thinking.

My husband, being the very intelligent and talented person that he is, could consider many aspects of any subject often times ending with a negative conclusion excluding any positive possibilities. Jim is a highly educated man with a broad scope of interests and an avid reader. He can talk by the hour on any subject if you can listen that long. Being in the field of education is a great calling for him as there is always an audience for the mammoth amount of information stored up in his brain. Fortunately, in my new commitment of trying to find a positive spin on subjects during our discussions, my new way of thinking began to dilute some of the harshness of always thinking on the down side.

Deliberately making this decision was a giant step forward in finding my own path out of my poor state of mental health, a condition I had now been living with for many years. I was discovering that there was a whole positive world happening around me that I had never recognized before. I had been so caught up in my own dark world that I was completely unable to recognize or participate in the good things that were happening daily around me. In fact, I was shocked. In every issue there had been lots of nays, leaving out the yeas, which give positive life force. Nor had I ever considered that they existed. That was to me a great revolutionary concept and discovery. Realizing that nays always are there, my focus now was going to be watching for the yeas of life. I so desired for life to be a performance with a balance.

Another discovery was that my new attitude was not reinforcing the negatives in my husband's mind. I was trying to become a counter balance by neutralizing as much as possible our negative thought patterns.

Attaining good mental health takes a lot of hard consistent work. It takes a daily practicing of your discoveries and remembering to do so until they become a habit.

Much later in time I came to realize that Someone had been at work all along answering the prayer which I had uttered during our dating days. What a relief to be experiencing some better mental health. I began to grasp the idea that I was truly getting better and the condition I had experienced for many years was fading. God in His love was leading me to understand some basic mental health principles. The encounter with that medical doctor was a truly a God planned event especially for me. God had used this medical specialist to help me set a different direction for my emotional self. Grasping the significance of that encounter was a slow catch-on to how God works in our lives.

Time had to take place before I understood that this doctor's encounter was another God whisper, letting me know that He is our caring and loving Heavenly Father. I did not connect that God whisper in my life until other God whispers started to enter my spiritual consciousness enabling me to connect some dots. Recognizing the real miracles that were taking place in my life, I now began to internalize the presence of a Divine

Savior who was doing what He had promised. However, I knew I had a lot of emotional and spiritual growth which still needed to take place. I felt some inner confidence growing that I was walking a path which was leading me out of that dark tunnel of depression that I had been traveling for a very long time. I was reminded of Psalm 11:16, "You have shown me the path of life." God was in the process of answering that prayer which I had uttered at least ten years prior. It took me a long time to catch on to that fact.

In trying to inform myself further to the world of psychology, I sought out related books and any written material that could offer information related to good mental health. Being mindful regarding the human brain and how it works, seeking information in order to discover any nuggets of truth that could be helpful, was really important to me. I needed some insights for myself and also for my father and his mysterious ways. Obscurity had surrounded his persona and I wanted to crack that mystery open also.

My own inherent immaturity delayed and interfered with the search for information and progress for these insights for living. There are definitely benefits to aging, bringing a maturity that can only be obtained through experience, education, and the development of our own spiritual dimension.

Mankind has a huge tendency to ignore the spiritual dimension thinking that education and experience outweighs all categories. Completely eliminating the importance of our relationship with Christ, our Creator, confusing the spiritual as a religion rather than a God connected relationship. It is important that these different areas work together as one; as one without the other a balance will never be provided. Without the spiritual as a foundation of this triad, a balance for living life will never be experienced.

Since man was created by God and has ignored His prescribed prescriptions we will never reap the results we are seeking. Leaving out this most important part of the treatment program will provide disappointing results. The spiritual provides a foundation for a better sense of a healthy self, that is, if we seek it. In my case, immaturity delayed some progress which I could have experienced sooner in my life. I was not aware of the work God was doing for me to bring about the emotional healing which I needed so badly. His work was not apparent much of the time but in snatches His involvement became evident. I have learned that this is one of His methods in teaching us how to walk by faith.

I cannot give credit to any medication for improvement, since none was available to me. I'm aware there are medications available which do help in cases of chemical imbalances. For those who have that kind of problem, thankfully there are medical treatments available making the difference between being able to function or not being able to face their day. My situation was circumstantial. There were these very challenging events which had taken place while as a youth and I had been totally unequipped emotionally to deal with them.

With these new insights growing in my mind, I was able to look forward to and already beginning to experience a different kind of future.

Summer Trips

EVERY SUMMER WE WOULD RETURN TO ALBERTA and back to the farm where I grew up. Jim insisted that we make the return trips since we were the ones who moved away. We agreed that family ties were very important and we wanted the children to know their grandparents. After we had made that seventeen hundred mile trip fifty times we stopped counting. Sometimes as a family we made the trip twice a year. On occasion Jim did not go so I would travel with the children by either bus or train.

I always appreciated Jim's push to make these annual trips when it was not his blood family we were visiting. I respected his effort and his desire to make it all happen for the benefit of us all, and benefit we did. That was what really mattered. He often referred to the "Cat in the Cradle." (A father who had no time for his growing son and in turn the son when grown had no time for the father). Jim did not want this to be his legacy. This was a very honorable motive on his part. However, there was certainly a side benefit for him as he loved the outdoors and Alberta provided plenty of opportunities for those experiences.

One of these outdoor experiences involved Jim hiking through the mountains all by himself. Hiking from Lake Louise down through rough mountainous terrain exiting the mountain range into the foothills west of our farm. He relates the story of meeting up with wolverines and crossing a river with his on the spot hand-made raft which popped apart as he was trying to cross this mountain stream. Rapid flowing water had stressed the ropes beyond their capacity to hold together.

Early one morning I drove him to his jumping off point located in Banff National Park. We both rode the gondola lift to the top of the mountain as I wanted to see him start his mountain hike. He was carrying his rifle, small axe, rope, and dried food supplies in his backpack as he walked off into the high altitude terrain.

Hiking solo through rough wilderness is not the best of ideas, however, when Jim makes his mind up there is no stopping him. Mother was so worried about this adventure she was convinced he would be devoured by some wild animal or get lost in the rugged wilderness. I could not worry as Jim was Jim. Going through a lot of preparation before commencing, he had given this hike a lot of thought.

Leaving the mountains he reunited with his previously stashed redesigned canoe with pontoons added for stability. Hidden among bushes close to a white water stream he planned to use it to navigate back to the western border of our farm. However, his trip ended with one end of the canoe being bashed in as it collided with a large boulder as he was trying to move through some rapids. Being able to disembark the disabled craft and wading through fast moving water he managed to remove himself and the canoe from this mountain stream.

Needless to say, the return home went differently than he had planned. Finding himself not very far from the forestry ranger station, he made his way there. Unbelievably, a friend of the family who just happened to be in the area was able to give him a ride back to the farm.

Upon arriving back at the farm he was a sight to behold, along with a smell that only one who hasn't showered for a week understands. I expected that he would not have shaven. His boots were all but worn out with blisters covering the soles of his feet. He seemed so thrilled with his big adventure in spite of all of the encountered obstacles I couldn't help but comment by saying "with all those blisters you still call this fun". Obviously my idea of fun was different than his.

Jim was initiated to the mountain wilderness a couple of years before we met. Deer and moose hunting trips with friends he met through his college professorship, birthed the hunting interest. He was totally undaunted by the exposure to its winter harshness. Wading through the deep snow, dressing for the extreme cold, and carrying his heavy rifle over his shoulder was an exhilarating experience. This made him feel very much alive and earned the nickname, "Jungle Jim."

Another mountain experience took place one week before our wedding almost causing him to lose his life while taking high school seniors on a mountain climbing expedition. A senior outing was a tradition at the very end of the school term.

Jim was in charge this fair and sunny day. They headed west by carpooling to mountain country. Spotting a lower profile peak than what it was surrounded by, but also didn't look to be as rugged as others seemed like a good choice for the day's adventure. The choice and decision was made to climb.

Orientation was given to the students, explaining some guidelines for all to be aware of. The go ahead was given and everyone started their ascent. Everything seemed to be in order and quite routine. Some students were climbing faster than others and some moved along much slower. Jim was to be the follower of the last one climbing.

Finally, reaching the acme most had already started their descent down the mountain side. As planned Jim was staying with the slower climbers. While they were still ascending, but close to the peak, a cloud moved in causing them to become directionally disorientated. Mother nature had stepped in to change this fair weather sunny day with a low level hanging cloud that brought complete confusion.

When deciding to turn back, Jim and two girls started to descend the wrong side of the mountain without realizing it. Instead of being able to see where they had just walked from, they were climbing down the backside. On that side they were faced with waterfalls, rugged rock formations, and cliffs. Their only way out seemed to be to slide down water chutes where their clothes got shredded from rocky outcrops and fallen sticks which had accumulated in the chutes. Even their shoes and boots became destroyed. Once they entered a chute the water carried them along and there was no stopping.

Just before darkness they found themselves at the base of the mountain, soaking wet and suffering from hypothermia in that crisp mountain air. Since they were already suffering from the cold in their wet condition and falling temperatures, survival till sunrise could have been a real disaster, with no extra jackets, sweaters or blankets. At this altitude freezing temperatures are normal even in June.

Upon their walking out of this unfortunate descent a calamity had been averted, but more than that they received a huge shout of relief and welcome from the rest of the group. Some horseback riders who had ridden upon the scene had joined in on the waiting. A big discussion had been taking place regarding search and rescue, perhaps a helicopter when daylight appeared. Fortunately, they had made their way out before darkness set in avoiding the disastrous effects of hypothermia and no rescue had to be made.

The next day Jim came to visit me at the farm looking as white as a sheet. I took one look at him and I asked "What is wrong?" He proceeded to fill me in on the happenings of the previous day, the emotional and physical trauma he and the two girls had experienced. One girl had completely panicked thinking that they were not going to make it back to the group and went into hysteria. Their shoes and clothes were shredded by the chutes and debris. When they reached the base of the mountain a huge echo of welcome and relief on the faces of their co-climbers were loudly demonstrated. Physical warmth had been restored by blankets and car heaters. Obviously, this experience had provided much more drama for the class outing than had been expected.

After our move to Wisconsin, my first trip back to Alberta was with our ten and a half month old baby girl. I would be traveling by myself along with the baby by railway while Jim remained in Milwaukee to teach summer school. He would be following about six weeks later by driving our Volkswagen, and then we would do the return trip together.

Jim drove me and our baby downtown to the Milwaukee Railway Station one mid-afternoon. I thought I had packed well and was ready for this two and half day train trip. As we said our goodbyes we talked about the rest of the summer and the plans which we had when we would see each other again after summer school was over.

I boarded the train, found a seat suitable for the two of us and proceeded to get to know the travelers around me. As it turned out a number of older ladies were traveling together. Visiting with these very friendly ladies would have been a pleasant experience except our daughter was being very wiggly and fully stimulated. In the meantime, my shopping bag which carried our immediate supplies disintegrated right before my eyes.

I should have known that a paper shopping bag would not be adequate for long distance traveling. Thinking that I had adequately prepared for this trip I was feeling embarrassed. At the same time I was wondering how I was going to harness all of our supplies with this bag disaster on my hands. Toys were landing on the floor along with the snacks I had packed. This wiggly kid certainly was not sleepy but very much awake, being stimulated by everything that exists in new surroundings.

All I can say is the Lord bless all the mature ladies who come to the aid of those young things that don't know what they are doing. These ladies were like magicians. Before I knew it, I had all the bags needed to go around the world twice. Their pity and generosity were much appreciated.

After I finally got my act together, the remainder of the trip went well. I definitely made some mental notes to myself about traveling with a small child. The immediate challenge I had was keeping her entertained for the remainder of the two and a half day trip.

We both adjusted to sleeping in those reclining seats. We had a couple of transfers, one in Winnipeg, the other in Calgary, but all went well in spite of a rocky beginning. My father met us at the depot with his red Ford pickup. This tiring trip had come to an end and I could let this wiggly kid do all the running her heart desired.

A memorable event occurred that summer. My mother and I along with my grandmother planned a berry picking trip to the foothills of the Rockies. Since this was my first visit after our daughter's birth and their first time of meeting this toddler, this trip enabled all to go together as four generations of women. We picked our wild blueberries with handmade pickers which mother had made from empty soup cans. She would solder nails to the can's rim making a handy tool for picking small berries on short bushes.

The wild berry patch had proven to be a good one so we picked until we were ready for a break. Being satisfied with our full buckets, we had lunch. We sat there in the woods in the middle of the berry patch, anchoring ourselves on a fallen log for a stool. We had buttered sandwich bread in our picnic basket and filled it with those freshly picked blueberries. As we sat on those logs eating our blueberry sandwiches we enjoyed every minute of our shared togetherness. We reminisced and laughed while my mother and grandmother enjoyed my daughter's exploring her new surroundings.

All the effort it had taken to travel back to Alberta that summer was well worth it. That berry picking outing was the last time that four generations of women could be together. The day was short-lived and passed quickly but is a golden memory for me.

One year later I found myself traveling again on a Greyhound bus with our daughter. This time she was a two year old and still wiggly. I was traveling from Alberta to Medford, Oregon to meet Jim who had been on a six week science stipend from the Oregon State University.

We had driven from Wisconsin to Canada together in our Volkswagen. After being there for a week, Jim needed to then travel on to southern Oregon without us. This gave me a six week visit with my family, which they loved.

This bus trip involved shorter time but was more taxing. Our daughter, being under two, could have a free seat if one was available. Our luck this time was a full bus, even at night time there was no seat available for her.

Leaving Alberta at eight o'clock in the morning, arriving in southern Oregon the next afternoon around three o'clock, made for a long tedious thirty-six hour trip- especially at night. I noticed many travelers falling asleep and leaning on each other even though they were strangers. The guy next to me did his share of leaning and I easily returned the gesture. Everyone was so sleepy they were not mindful of how their physical positions were changing. If another body was keeping you propped up, mindfulness was not part of the scene. Somehow, I managed to keep my daughter on my lap without dropping her on the floor. Needless to say, when this trip came to an end upon arriving at our Medford, Oregon, destination, no regrets came to mind.

Reuniting with my husband after a six week separation, we were ready for our lives to return to normal. His time of study with the university had come to an end. We proceeded to study a road map trying to decide on the shortest and quickest way to get to Salt Lake City, where we could pick up a major highway going east.

Jim made his decision, choosing a road that went through northern California and northern Nevada.

This so called road eventually became a grassy trail through the desert. No road signs, no warnings existed, or anything giving any indication as to where we actually were or when services would be available next. Fortunately, we had a full tank of gas and the air was not hot, as we found ourselves driving through this desert wilderness during the night time hours. We had not made proper preparation for desert wilderness travel. Later, as I thought about the dangers that could have presented themselves, we felt fortunate. We were also traveling with our two year old. On the map this appeared to be much more of a road than it turned out to be.

Surprisingly, this arid environment was inhabited with plenty of rabbits and owls. At first we tried to dodge the rabbits but there were so many we finally quit, cringing every time the car went thump. That thumping happened so often we decided that there had to be a major rabbit plague. Even the owls were not able to keep the rabbit population under control.

We had driven all night through this desolate land arriving outside of Salt Lake City with the Volkswagen engine continuing to perform on gas fumes. This route was obviously not the wisest route to take, in hindsight. With no warning signs regarding the primitive road conditions that we would be entering, we had not anticipated that we would be facing these hazardous conditions.

As for the remainder of our trip back to the Midwest, thankfully, there was a lot less drama except for leaving our daughter's sweater at a restaurant in Greely, Colorado.

As we made our return trips from Wisconsin to Alberta we both became so enamored with the beauty of the area enjoying it fully together. Even though I had lived in Alberta I had never had traveled around the province. That was something that my parents were unable to do.

Banff National Park owned real treasures for the eye to behold. Lake Louise, Moraine Lake, Johnson Canyon, along with the town of Banff with its scenic location, were our favorites until we journeyed to Jasper National Park and later to Watertown Lakes National Park. We decided that we didn't have a favorite after all as they were all so magnificent.

Jim had grown to love everything there was to love about Alberta. He had done a lot exploring during those three years of his teaching career and missed it a lot. Returning each year gave him the opportunity to relive some of the experiences which he had not been able to fulfill. He had gone on moose hunting trips with his Canadian friends, taken mountain drives and hiked through some of the wilderness areas. The beauty of the mountains and lakes were unmatched. He couldn't seem to absorb enough of them. He had lots of reasons for keeping his promise for the family to return every year if it was at all possible. With Jim and I both being in education facilitated our ability to have meaningful times during for our summer trips.

My family was hugely disappointed when we moved out of province. For them traveling was out of the question. My father had his problems and fear of the unknown was a crippling factor for my mother's mindset. She was sure disaster was around the corner if it was beyond her mind to accept.

Understanding my parents and their limitations we never expected them to visit Milwaukee and they never did. Our goal was to maintain family relations as much as possible and also have the children experience country living since we were residing in a large city.

Traveling to and fro provided extraordinary experiences for our family to reminisce over when we are together. Laughter always comes after someone saying "I remember the time when---."

In the beginning all five of us traveled in our Volkswagen car until space demanded something larger. We would travel all night while the children slept giving us some peace but also wanting to get the miles behind us. We would make stops during the day to give them some exercise time. During those times we would stop at the A and W Root Beer and be served by the car hops, ordering hamburgers and fries. Usually there was a play picnic area where the children could let off some steam before reloading the car and moving on. For short breaks we would look for some picnic areas where we could enjoy some snacks or find an ice cream place. After driving all night we would stop at a restaurant for a breakfast of pancakes and orange juice.

Motels were never a part of the budget. When we chose not to drive all night we would stop at primitive campgrounds which seemed to be the only thing available then along the routes we traveled. Sometimes we slept in the tent, in the car, or on the ground in a sleeping bag. Even picnic tables work as a bed. Open air sleeping is an experience all of its own. We have slept in freshly harvested wheat fields of Montana, the big sky country. The awareness of nature becomes very real when the night sky decorated with the heavenly stars becomes your night cover.

Isaiah 45:18: "Thus says the Lord who created the heavens, God Himself made the earth and formed it, He established it, He created it not in vain but to be inhabited. I am the Lord and there is no one else."

We would vary our routes as much as possible since we were repeatedly headed for the same destination. The first trips we made we traveled the northern US route. Leaving Milwaukee we headed for Minnesota and North Dakota onward to southern Montana. Arriving at Glendive was our turning point to head north to Havre a real western style town where Jim stood in the middle of the main street singing very loudly, " I'm an old cow hand from the Rio Grande," while at the same time bending his knees in a mock squat and lifting his cowboy hat in a wave motion. Needless to say we all said to ourselves "We don't know this man." Jim was obviously sick of being in the car and was giving us some comic relief. It has always been in Jim's nature to create drama wherever he goes. This was just one of those occasions. Being the director of stage productions at his high school, this fit his personality perfectly.

After getting something to eat we were on the road again aiming for Sweet Grass which would be the border crossing into Canada.

Other times we would take the southern route from Minneapolis across Iowa to the Black Hills, onward to South Dakota and the badlands. Seeing buffalo and antelope in open range gave us a thrill. Of course we all had to sing together "Home on the Range". Continuing on crossing the northwest corner of Wyoming, we would turn north aiming for western Montana. Following the mountains northward would provide some of the most beautiful vistas treating us to lots of scenic variety as we traveled.

Another chosen route included traveling across the southern prairie provinces. Traveling north from Grand Forks, North Dakota we would head north to Winnipeg, Manitoba then picking up the Canadian Highway Number One going west. Since we were making so many trips, Jim always had a suggestion to vary each route somewhat so that we could keep our trips as fresh as possible. We would try to work in some detours along the way in an effort to provide some variation to those seemingly unending roadways.

Silent Tears

Our early day's cars were not equipped with air-conditioning. Since the hot summer months were the months we had to travel, wind from open car windows along with those high summer temperatures became very fatiguing. Our solution was to roll all of the car windows down about four inches. That gave us lots of cross ventilation without drying out our skin and turning our hair into straw. It wasn't like air-conditioning but it worked. That trick greatly improved our comfort level.

Each trip we made included some outstanding event that ironed itself into our memory bank. Some were more impressive than others but all were enough to keep us from forgetting the details.

One such memory occasion occurred when traveling west from Winnipeg on the Canadian Highway Number One. This stop involved a stay at a campground outside of Brandon, Manitoba.

We managed to find a campground just before night fall and were glad to be off the road after putting in our long driving hours. Being seven months pregnant, I was plenty ready to call it a day.

We pitched our large old second hand tent, stabilizing it with those wonderful tent stakes that barely go into the ground without a sledge hammer. This tent was weighty being made of course heavy canvas. A canvas floor added to the poundage of our nightly abode as well. By the time we got it up and staked we felt like we had a day's worth of exercise. Finally being able to roll out our sleeping bags everything was now ready for a good night's sleep. The last thing we did before reclining was to eat from our cooler.

Four o'clock in the morning I was awakened by the most disturbing claps of thunder I had ever heard from a thunderstorm. Each clap was like an explosion with very little of a break in between each loud boom. Now that I'm wide awake, I said to myself this is no normal storm. I awakened Jim trying to get him to tune his mind into this approaching storm. What I got was what I call the typical male response. "Oh stop worrying everything is going to be alright, go back to sleep, it's only a storm passing through."

To me there was no way I was going to be able to go back to sleep with these very loud explosive boomers. Within seconds of those thoughts; the wind hit. The tent was literally lifting off the ground and I was thinking for sure we were going to roll up in that tent and blow away. By now, not only was Jim awake but also the two children. All of us piled together on the rising side in an effort to hold down the tent. Just as quickly as the wind hit us, the wind was gone. The whole wind- blast had only lasted maybe a minute or so. The wind stopped as quickly as it had started. The rumbles were subsiding and calm was filling the air. Being able to breathe a little easier, feeling that now the storm had now passed, we could retire again with confidence. However, there was no sleep in our eyes after that nerve wracking awakening. After some middle of the night chatter, before long we were able to let go of that sudden unexpected sleep interruption.

Upon rising the next morning we learned a tornado had gone through the area. Two airplanes at nearby airport had been destroyed along with some other damages that were less severe. I was surprised. I knew that it was an unusual storm but I had not thought in terms of a tornado. Jim didn't make any comments, which was better that he didn't.

On that same trip taking the same route on the return back to Wisconsin, we heard these unfriendly sounds coming from the Volkswagen engine that spelled serious trouble. We made it to a garage but learned that they could not help us. They said they didn't work on these small foreign cars. The only solution was to call a tow truck who could take us to a garage that did service foreign cars. The only problem was that foreign car repair shop was eighty five miles down the road putting us back in Brandon, Manitoba, our tornado town. So we found ourselves back in Brandon for a different reason.

Our tow bill was seventy five dollars and we had to pay cash out of our pocket since we didn't have towing insurance. The engine problem turned out to be not serious after all. The part and the repair bill totaled about twenty five dollars. There was some small part in the engine that didn't function correctly. Having to pay a seventy five dollar tow bill for a minor twenty five dollar part, hurt a lot psychologically. We decided from then on we would always carry towing insurance regardless whether the vehicle was new or an older one.

Three weeks after arriving home in Milwaukee our youngest son was born. That same day Jim ended up in the hospital with hepatitis. We were in the same hospital four floors apart. Jim didn't get to see his newborn son until he was nearly a week old.

During our traveling days with our Volkswagens, having owned more than one at different times, one stop we made for the night was at a campground in Yellowstone National Park where we were assigned a site under a tall tree. That was okay with us as the shade from the tree would provide shelter from the sun if we needed it.

The handyman that Jim is, he had built a number of framed screens that could be assembled to form a triangular tent like space to anchor to the top of the Volkswagen. When it was open it was a perfect space for giving us a sleeping facility above ground away from ants and bugs etc. To reach this sleep space, Jim had built a ladder that was permanently bolted to the rear end of the car for security. Jim's ladder made getting up and down a convenient effort. For privacy we threw a large canvas over the whole unit removing that concern. He also made a way to close the entrance so that our daughter could not tumble out providing that needed safety measure. When traveling, everything collapsed down to a flat thin object to reduce wind resistance.

When camping, the rising sun gives you your morning wake-up call. On this particular camping morning after doing some yawning, stretching, and peering around at our surroundings, we discovered that a black bear had made himself at home right above us in the tall tree. We suddenly became highly motivated to break camp, repack, and leave that campsite while the bear just continued sleeping. Apparently he wanted to sleep in but he cut ours short. We appreciated the consideration of the bear in not trying to share our sleeping quarters with us.

During those trips we had our share of flat tires and burned out ball bearings. We even lost a bag of luggage from the car top carrier just before going over a highway overpass south of Winnipeg. Fortunately, we saw the bag of luggage go tumbling down the bank. An unusual sound caught our attention that something was amiss. Bringing the vehicle to a stop before we had gone past the point of no return, Jim managed to crawl down over the bank and retrieve the wayward piece of luggage. One of us in the car was going to have clothes to wear this summer after all.

Jim doubled down his effort to secure the rest of the luggage, making sure that the tie downs were good and tight so that we wouldn't be having a repeat act of this sort.

Traveling with animals provided some unique, memorable, and learning experiences. We traveled with the kid's pet cat that learned to create his own adventures. While we slept in our tent he would do some hiking on his own. One morning Charlie was missing. After many calls using his name, he showed up approaching us through the field of weeds. Thumper, a small rabbit given to the children by my mother crossed the

Silent Tears

Canadian border with us on a return trip. We hid her under a blanket as we talked to the border guard. That gift multiplied faster than we were prepared for. We were naïve about the speed of rabbit production. The largest animal we ever transported was our daughter's horse.

We had just purchased a small horse for our daughter. Needing a way to transport this mare we started looking for a trailer. Jim found this one horse trailer that needed a lot of restoration. Being the do it yourself kind of man, he was totally undaunted with the prospect. Even though his vocation was in education he loved having physical projects. He was a natural when it came to using his hands and tools.

When he had refurbished the rusty old trailer with a new floor, paint job with flames on the sides, and new tires it was unrecognizable as being the same piece. Storage for tack, hay, and grain was also added on the sides. On the road the storage lids became our table when we stopped for snacks and drinks. This trailer was truly one of a kind.

Thinking that the kids would enjoy riding their horse on the many available acres we made the decision to take the horse with us to my parent's farm. We had removed the mare from the city stable for the summer and had taken her to our summer property. Not wanting to leave her alone while away the simple solution was to take her with us. When I think back about all of this, it doesn't seem so simple to my current state of mind.

Being that this was a new experience for our family, we knew that we had to do some planning. When stopping at night, how were we going to manage that? Decision was---at the wayside stops, unload and exercise, then tie the horse to a tree. The kids were to pull out their sleeping bags and sleep next to her on the grassy banks. We needed to keep her company so that she wouldn't become nervous and lonesome in the new environs. Wayside stops along the highways were not so regulated at that time. Today that would never work.

International border crossing would be another obstacle to plan for. We did our research finding out that we had to have a health certificate dated no more than ten days prior of border crossing. Off to the local veterinary clinic we went to have her inspected. We received the certificate we needed. This didn't seem so overwhelming. We felt well prepared for our international crossing.

Space was another issue. Our two boys were now pre-teen and our daughter was a teenager. Our equipment for traveling was this one horse trailer towed by an old blue Chevy car. Jim had managed to purchase this vehicle feeling that if driven properly it could do what we needed it to do. That need was to pull this loaded trailer, plus luggage and five bodies seventeen hundred miles one way or double it for the return trip. Our family had expanded in ways that were new to us. Traveling with the cat and the rabbit seemed a lot simpler. Now we had the horse, plus our kids who were older and bigger. Space now became a serious consideration.

We had always traveled with limited supplies but with enough. In planning for those needs six tee shirts per person along with six pairs of socks and underwear seemed like a good place to start. Jeans were limited to three pair along with one hooded sweatshirt. Each had a sleeping bag and a pillow. A Woolworth's plastic bag with handles for each held a towel, toothbrush and paste, shampoo, and comb, so each had their own when stopping at a campground.

Those ninety nine cent plastic bags from the now non-existent Woolworth Dime Stores were indispensable. They would hold all toiletries needed for personal care when stopping at road side campsites with their primitive showers. They were affordable and durable enough to last through the rigors of a two to six week family vacation without busting out at the seams. I should have had those for that disastrous train trip with our one year old.

Space was always a premium for five passengers traveling in medium sized, never new vehicles. Packing took some serious planning with definite limitations. Each family member was allowed a small suitcase for their summer wardrobe plus that sleeping bag and pillow. We would plan to go to the Laundromat once a week to catch up with the clean clothes supply.

This system worked for us. It was simple enough to help us maintain the feeling of being organized, yet giving us enough supplies to meet our needs when on the road and visiting family for extended periods of time. For all of our summer trips I used the same formula to facilitate vacation planning time.

When we were finally loaded we could have passed as cousins of the Beverly Hillbillies. Our old blue Chevy was bulging with the trunk lid hardly closing. Our horse, Bambi, was in the trailer along with the tack needed. A grain and hay supply was stored in the trailer side boxes ready to serve this hungry equine. A last minute idea was to take along the dune buggy which Jim attached to the horse trailer tail gate. With that buggy we were really loaded. Jim had his own recreational visions for using that vehicle on those many farm acres.

Everything went as planned without hitches until we arrived at the Canadian customs crossing at Cardston, Alberta. The customs agent kindly informed us that our horse would have to be inspected by their customs veterinary, as well. Even though we had our horse's health certificate she still had to have the secondary inspection. That sounded okay until the border agent informed us the veterinary wasn't available on Sundays. That fact had never entered our minds. We had assumed our certificate was enough. We could have their vet come up from Lethbridge and not wait the twenty fours until he was on duty. There would be a fee charged for his weekend services. The fee was not going to be $2.98 either. Their weekend services were a lot of money.

Feeling very frustrated, we sat in the car thinking about what our next step should be. Within moments a young cowboy dressed in all of his unmistakable country western attire, boots, rugged jeans, leather vest and the broad rimmed high crowned hat along with that unmistakable wrangler swagger approached our car. He had just discovered that he too had the same problem we were having. He was parked behind us with a trailer load of horses. He was headed to the Calgary Stampede and needed to get there that day. He offered a suggestion. He would have the border vet called and we could split the fee. We agreed. Sitting there for a couple hours sounded better than a long twenty four hour wait.

Those two hours of waiting between the United States and Canada provided some excitement for the kids and entertainment for the border agents. This early July weather was sunny and hot. Keeping Bambi cool and watered in the trailer during the wait was fun to the kids. They ran back and forth between the two countries lugging their buckets of water. This was definitely a unique experience for them. None of their friends would have this kind of tale to tell upon returning home at the end of their summer vacation.

Remembering there would be a return trip, avoiding the border on a Sunday might be a good plan.

One year later my mother offered our kids her half Arab mare. We were involved with a 4H Horse Club project and mother imagined a use for her no longer needed mare. This mare had not been ridden or handled much in fourteen years.

This mare had also been a free-range horse for most of those years with little human attention during that time. There was going to be some training and retraining which was going to require time. Hopefully, there would be enough of that in order to be ready for transportation from Alberta to Wisconsin. That also meant hauling that horse trailer again.

After a family discussion a decision was made in favor of this new adventure. The kids were excited, Jim was game for it, and the idea didn't daunt me that much since I had grown up with horses. We had worked through the hauling process the prior year so preparation seemed much simpler this time around.

Simpler was what we thought until mother found out we would be traveling one way with an empty horse trailer. Her request was to stop at the University of Manitoba in Winnipeg at the Agricultural Division to pick up a couple of yearling lambs. These lambs were of an experimental breed. These were supposed to be a litter raising breed, imported from Russia. She had done the research and was hot on her idea. Needless to say, simpler became adjusted a bit.

Simpler also was affected by a woman border patrol. She wanted to know what we planned to do with this empty horse trailer. Jim, being the very wordy person that he is, told the whole story. This officer firmly informed us that we couldn't haul commercially across Canada without a commercial license. That is when the lamb idea got nixed, until a male officer gave us a knowing look that this was a private deal and not a commercial one. Our interpretation was to go on as planned. We did just that and mother got her lambs.

Horses are known for their long term memory. Mother's little Arabian mare had maintained hers. She remembered what a grain bucket looked like, how a halter felt, although she hesitated a bit. She even let us load her into the trailer while still at the range sight. It wasn't until we got her back to the farm that rebellion set in.

Continual friendly persuasion with a rump rope was needed, to remind her who was in charge, when it came to trailer loading. She had tried full-fledged rebellion in that department but in time decided the battle wasn't worth it. We had finally been able to convince her that she had nothing to be nervous about, winning her confidence.

Our two week vacation had come to an end. We were feeling confident about traveling with our new companion and wiser about when to cross the international border along with a current health certificate.

Being on the road again as a family involved the usual anticipation of experiences which we had grown accustomed to becoming almost routine. Sleeping on the ground under the stars by a tree next to our equine friend, keeping her company, had become a normal activity.

Big Sky Montana seems to last forever and North Dakota doesn't seem much shorter either. By the time we would reach the Minnesota border we felt like we were almost home.

We always tried to travel as a family. There were times circumstances didn't accommodate that. I took two train trips from Milwaukee to Olds, Alberta with the three children when they were still very young. These trips are ones I wouldn't even consider now, but then it seemed to be the answer of the day.

Our youngest was twenty one months old, the middle one just over three years and the oldest, a little more than six. This particular trip had a midnight beginning. Not much sleep was going to take place as train boarding time was one o'clock in the morning.

For this early departure we managed to gather ourselves together in an organized enough fashion to make the half hour trip to the station. The children were in such a sleepy, dazed state they weren't very aware of what was really happening.

We purchased my ticket as travelers under the age of seven had a free rate. We said our early morning goodbyes, boarded the train, and found our seats for the first lap of our trip. The children soon fell asleep after getting ourselves settled. Arrival time in Minneapolis was to be around seven that morning after a long slow ride. Surprisingly, even late at night the train makes lots of stops in small towns.

Silent Tears

We had an hour and a half to make our change from the arrival to the departing one giving us plenty of time to transfer. These two trains were railed at the same station creating a convenience for a mature human dragging along three immature ones that had been deprived a normal night's sleep.

Our newly boarded train was headed for Fargo, North Dakota where we would be making another transfer to connect with a rail going north to Winnipeg. This change didn't take place at a depot but in the middle of nowhere with open fields and tall grass surrounding the entire area. There wasn't even a farm house insight. Everyone disembarked walking out onto a mixed gravel and grassy area designated for standing until the north bound train was available. The children became wide eyed with this new experience being aware that they were among a lot of strangers. Entertainment was no problem.

This next lap of the trip went well until little brother threw up on big sister's paper dolls. Now, from time to time, little brother is reminded by adult sister of the thoughtful performance on her dolls, with humor of course.

In Winnipeg, arriving and departure were at two different stations. Shuffling from one station to the other was an act all of its own. Dealing with the disembarking crowd demanded that I keep our youngest on a leash so that he didn't get swept up in the anxious to get somewhere walkers. My hands were always full of supplies so there was a lot to juggle in a short period of time. Besides my hands being full of bags and a little kid on the leash, I was also trying to keep track of the other two. I felt the need to keep them in sight in case they also got caught up in the crowd stream becoming disoriented and separated. Being aware was necessary for everyone's safety.

With disembarking completed a taxi was now needed to transfer us across town to the west bound station. Managing to make our next connection in a relatively smooth manner, we boarded, found seats together, and fell asleep after a long exhausting day.

Next mid afternoon my father met us at the station in his blue Chevy pickup. What a relief to be off the train.

⁓

One year later, the children and I made a repeat trip by rail. This time the scheduling created a whole new set of circumstances presenting challenges which I didn't look forward to but not so daunting that I wasn't willing to go.

Scheduling the details was a nightmare unfolding. Our schedule for leaving Milwaukee was mid afternoon, which would be good, arriving in Winnipeg seven o'clock next morning still sounded alright. Departing to go west would not take place until eleven o'clock that night. That meant there would be a fourteen hour layover in an unfamiliar city where I did not know anyone plus I would be dragging along three small children. How was I going to pass these long hours with children who sleep deprived, tired from traveling with no known place to restore ourselves?

Discovering that there was no alternative to this lousy schedule, I would travel anyway. The route from Milwaukee to Minneapolis was a repeat, but the grassy field connection on the North Dakota border had been eliminated.

After departing from Milwaukee and finally arriving in the Winnipeg depot at seven that morning we disembarked as normal then looked for some lockers to store our luggage for the day.

"Where is the city zoo and how can we get there?" I asked at an information counter. I was informed that there was a city bus a couple blocks away which would take us straight to the zoo. Knowing the ease of that was a great relief.

Silent Tears

We passed the day at the zoo, enjoying viewing animals from around the world. We watched the ducks and graceful swans paddle around on the ponds immersing their long necks and heads into the depth of the water feeding off the bottom. The children had the chance to play tag and tumble around barefoot in the freshly mown soft green grass. This was a very welcome change from the confinement of a rail car. We picnicked in the warm sunshine snacking on our overnight leftovers until our bags were empty.

My watch finally showed four o'clock. I decided we had better organize ourselves and head back to the depot. We still had to hire a taxi to make our connection with the west bound train namely the Canadian Pacific Railway. We had been at the zoo long enough, and it was time to sort out the remainder of the day.

We recovered our luggage from the lockers and flagged down a taxi which transported us across town to the connecting station. I purchased our west bound tickets. Children under seven could still go free. Our daughter who was now seven would have to pay half fare, still a good deal. As I'm paying the clerk, she informed me that there were men who hung around the station, and if any of them bothered us I was to let her know.

Quick surveillance showed a couple of old men sitting by themselves on those long wooden pew- like benches with their heads bowed in a sleeping posture quite unaware of life around them. They seemed to be in their own world at the moment and not at all threatening. I didn't give the subject another thought since having dinner was really on my mind.

I turned back to the clerk asking where a restaurant might be. She responded by pointing to a large restaurant sign above a wide stairway. Not thinking any negative thoughts or receiving any other warnings from the clerk, I headed that way entering a wide stairway. Before long I realized we had entered a very long tunnel with many pools of what looked like water. Realizing that this was not water but these homeless men were using this hallway to relieve themselves. I grabbed the kid's hands and shouted to them "Let's get out of here!" We ran the rest of the way through this long passage way. Apparently this rail depot had become a hang out place for homeless men.

Reaching the bottom of another large stairway we ascended to a receptionist's desk. A hostess greeted us with a smile and led us to a table. Now I was suddenly realizing we were in a whole different environment. It was the opposite of what we had just experienced.

Lovely music flooded the air-waves, deep wine colored velour chairs, plush carpeting, and white linen tablecloths were dressing every table. This was not exactly the kind of restaurant I had in mind. I'm thinking we are a motley bunch who spent the day at the zoo, plus in my mind I'm visualizing a pricey meal. All I wanted was some spaghetti for these three white linen mannerless children. Just a simple meal please. Before any waitress showed up I decided that it was time to vacate so we got up and walked out.

Outside and looking over my shoulder to see where we had just been, a very large lettered sign was advertising this ritzy hotel and restaurant. Relieved to be out of there, I continued to orient myself to the area. Spotting an Italian restaurant across the street with a sign in the window advertising spaghetti drew us like a magnet. At last dinner was a possibility which made our salivary glands flow. This atmosphere was going to be appropriate for us. Now we could finally relax enjoying a family style meal, filling the empty physical cavities before we had to deal with another long wait.

Spaghetti, good garlic bread with a salad satisfied us all to the fullest. Happy and satisfied, but physically tired, it was only seven o'clock, with another four hours to wait and a short walk across the street but no tunnel to journey through.

Boarding time finally came. We had used every distraction idea that came to mind to pass the time. Children never play very quietly so the homeless men were probably very happy when we left. We disturbed them more than they did us. They seemed to continue their resting posture in those hard wooden seats that furnished the depot. Apparently it was no issue with the rail station to have the homeless hanging out there.

Twenty four more hours spent with the rail system and my father was scheduled to meet us.

Our return trip that summer went more smoothly than the first lap. Everything was a repeat, except that we only had a six hour layover in Winnipeg. We broke that time up by going to see the movie "The Love Bug," at a nearby theater. For once, something was convenient. That gave us a nice break.

Our goals for these summer trips were simple enough in our minds. We wanted adventure, time with family, affordable trips, and new experiences for Jim and I as well as the children. Bringing that about took planning and the willingness to compromise so that the whole family would benefit.

Money was always in short supply. We managed to limit ourselves in our expenditures in order to make these activities possible. Jim had a good eye for buying used cars as well as the knowledge for their maintenance. We learned to manage on a lot less than luxury.

Learning to travel was a growing experience for the children. Once the car was loaded and we were on the road, the children knew they had a job to do, which was to entertain themselves. We learned to make up games, sing songs, and watch for themed subjects, such as counting the number of cars with a certain license plate. They also had their own travel bag with games included. They learned to never ask, "Are we there yet?" Once the last door was slammed on departure they knew time spent in the vehicle was going last a long time.

Selma J. Stroebel

Arriving at my parent's farm introduced a whole new set of activities. Reuniting with family was big but also a time of learning about nature, animal life, farm duties, and recreation. Mother was always actively medicating some under-the-weather creature which fascinated our daughter to no end. For children who lived in a large city with limited country experience, this was an eyes wide open gig.

Mother always had a project lined up for us all when we would arrive, knowing full well that Jim would be looking for something of that nature anyway. He had installed plumbing, a central heating system, and kitchen cabinets for her. One summer he built a garage using tent pallets which mother managed to find. They had originated from Banff National Park. How she found those was a symbol of mother's imaginary solution to a need. She was never short of ideas. Regardless, she got her garage and was very proud of Jim's work. Needless to say we were rarely idle while visiting family.

Tent camping with my aunt and uncle in the foot hills introduced our whole family to the foothill wilderness experiences and to God's concert hall. Becoming still enough to hear the true sounds of nature and aware of how much is missed by our senses because of our busy and noisy lifestyles pokes at your consciousness.

Night sounds become most intriguing. Gentle breezes brushing the quaking aspens seem to caress the soul while the rippling stream flowing over the rocks sounds like God's own violin section. Crickets become the choir while the whippoorwills perform their arias. The night owls bring an unmistakable rhythm all of their own. They are nature's drummers.

These summer family reunions also provided some favorite memories for cousin time spent together. Yes, these were the country experiences which only country settings can provide. Eating, sleeping together in tents, following their grandparents around, and learning about country life through their own eyes. Bringing vegetables and berries from mother's huge, one person managed garden, were delights of theirs. An armful of freshly pulled up carrots, delighted their spirits while also providing a healthy snack. Horseback riding was on that list too, as well as wading and go-carting adventures in the tributaries of Big Red. Exploring the beaver wetlands and their houses drew their curiosity like magnets. However, there was one activity that could only be experienced in the manner in which it was because of the uniqueness of the environment.

Our children and their cousin had their own outdoor theater near a bubbling spring where wild mink liked to fish for fingerlings. These times together as cousin time became etched in their long term memories. My husband had built a bridge connecting the two banks of the creek, offering a passage over the crystal-clear gently flowing water. An original setting that could not be out-matched, laying there in the shadow of a mixture of tall trees, providing mystical lighting, and stimulation for fertile imaginations.

Costumes were created from my parent's farm clothing; mother's faded straw hats and my father's worn and misshapen felts. Billy Goats Gruff and Hansel and Gretel were summer plays, we, as parents and grandparents attended. There were other presentations too. The cathedral seating was the moss covered ground on the creek bank that gave us an elevated view of the performances. And of course, the cast were non-professional performers, but all did a great job. Parents and grandparents gave credit to the cast members in generous amounts where credit was due, and to the director. Of course the director was the oldest member of the cast and probably the most bossy.

Jim and I agreed on the values which we wanted to bring to our family life and the legacy which we wanted to leave our children.

Selma J. Stroebel

We had both experienced a lot of turmoil in our respective families. We wanted to leave a different kind of heritage and legacy. We desired to break the negative cycle which had so plagued any effort for true and meaningful family relationships but instead had developed a tremendous amount of dysfunction. Maintaining healthy family connections was very important if possible. Our summer trips helped us accomplish those goals.

My own emotional well-being had greatly changed and the path out of my long term depression had brought long sought after relief, however, the concern which I had for my Mother and Father had not resolved itself by any measure. That still negatively affected me in ways that I still had not learned how to cope with. When I would allow myself to think of my parents and their situation, I would still literally become ill for a number of days. It was very difficult to deal emotionally with how I felt, plus I would end up with migraines. Needless to say, I continued to do a lot of mental blocking in order to cope with the emotions that still haunted me.

Saying our goodbyes became a nightmare every time we needed to return to Wisconsin. My Mother was convinced that each time we left this was going to be the last time she would ever see us again. Soon after we would arrive for each visit those thoughts would be going through her mind. This impeded her ability to enjoy our visit to the fullest. She kept these thoughts in the fore. You could easily see the strain of these thoughts expressed on her face. It was heart breaking to watch someone important to you be so unhappy and not enjoying her life. She had placed on my shoulders a responsibility for her happiness and that was a heavy weight to carry. My inability to do anything about it was continuing to be very emotionally draining. Today, with the knowledge which I have, a counselor would be involved for her sake.

Even though I knew there was nothing that could solve my parent's current situation, both Jim and I knew we were building positive memories and experiences for our children. They also were getting to know their grandparents and extended family members with an emotionally healthy connection that would be important in their future.

Following is an essay written by our youngest about his version of trips to his grandparents.

A Trip to Canada
By---John Stroebel

Every summer, our family takes its annual trip to Alberta, Canada to our grandmother's house which is nestled in the foothills of the Rocky Mountains. I can remember one year vividly. We always had a few soft pillows and blankets left aside from the packing to put in the back seat for extra comfort. On this particular trip we lived in Milwaukee and we would leave from there and would drive to a little truck stop and eat our first meal on the road. The truck stop was just over the Wisconsin-Minnesota border. I can remember clearing the St. Croix River and going into the St. Paul area, where the traffic would always get increasingly heavy. Rush hour usually hit about 5:00. As we entered Minneapolis, I can remember the sound barriers around the express way to keep the noise pollution away from the residential area. The sound barriers looked like the walls of an ancient medieval castle.

About that time it was getting dark, we would stop and change drivers because my dad had been driving all day. My mom usually took over and drove. Since I didn't have my driver's license, I would usually stay up all night and keep the drivers awake. I can always remember going through the Dakotas because it always took the longest to get through. It seemed like a million years. I can always remember Bismarck, North Dakota because it meant that we were half way through North Dakota. The thing that I remember most about North Dakota, are the Bad Lands.

Selma J. Stroebel

I always liked to look out the window of the car. As far as I could see there were trenches and gorges that looked like an endless maze.

Then came Montana, which we usually passed through at night. This particular time we did. After Montana, we came to the US-Canadian Border. Once at the Canadian border, we would pull up to the gate and the officer on duty would ask us some questions and let us pass through. Then off to Calgary, Alberta we would go. By this time it was the second day and we were anxious to get to our grandmother's house. After Calgary it was 80 miles to our grandmother's house. I could start to see the mountains on the horizon. You could see the white snow caps on top of them. The snow caps looked like caps on giants all walking in a row with their arms interlocking so we couldn't see their arms at all. As we got closer to our grandmother's house, it started to get hilly and the mountains started to get closer. I could tell we were about two miles from our grandmother's house because when we drove on top of a particular hill we could see the mountains clearly. The road we were on went straight into the mountains like a knife cutting into its soul.

As we drove down the road to my grandmother's house, I can never forget the feeling I got when we drove down the road. The trees were always in a straight line on both sides of the road like a path that cuts through tall grass. The sun shone onto the trees acting like an umbrella only letting a few rays shine through like lasers. As the wind blew, moving the tips of the trees, the rays danced across the car and the road giving an effect that only the imagination could picture.

As we got closer we had to drive down a hill that my grandmother lived at the bottom of. She lived in a valley that was beautiful and rich. The hay was green and very lush. As we drove to the gate down the long driveway you could see the gophers running on their hind legs through the cow pasture. From there you could see the house with the mountains looking down upon it with loving arms around it.

Silent Tears

(This is an essay which our youngest son wrote for a school assignment in junior high.)

Memories

Memories are a special house
We build inside ourselves
Where love and laughter linger
Where all our past life dwells.

Sometimes we have a need
To draw upon that store
Reliving happy times
To feel that warmth once more.

Wherever we may travel
This house is always there
Helping to blend the old and new
To build on, grow, and share.

This house can never get too full
It just grows from floor to floor
Because the joy of making memories
Will always be dreaming more.

Significance Almost Missed

THIS RETURN TRIP TO ALBERTA presented an occasion on the first day of our arrival that would be considered routine and not unusual. This simple scene could occur in anyone's household but it turned out to be a scene that caused an abrupt challenge to my thinking. I had almost missed the significant moments that unfolded before me and was slow to grasp the depth of all it meant. The occasion had seared itself into my memory haunting me with the need to record it for future preservation. That restlessness gnawed at my innermost self for many years to come. There was a story and it was up to me to tell it.

My home town of Sundre is a beautiful small town nestled in the foothills of the Canadian Rockies. It is the last town to drive through before entering the forested foothills and the mountains. Approaching Sundre, you are at the top of a big hill looking down on the town located in the Red Deer River Valley with snow capped mountains on the western horizon. I enjoyed this scene every morning as I rode the school bus to school. I really didn't treasure this beauty until I had moved away and returned for visits. Too bad we have to age before we value what we have or had. However, this was my home town where I had attended school for a portion of my education. Our family farm was located seven miles north of town, with the Red Deer River bordering it on its western side.

We had just driven the seventeen hundred miles before arriving. My parents and maternal grandparents had been anxiously waiting for our arrival. They had never met our youngest son, being born after our previous visit and now nine months old.

The children were inspected closely for changes that had taken place since our last visit. Our daughter age five, had retained memories of prior visits so was delighted to see family again and be the object of love and attention. The middle one's memory wasn't that clear but eventually warmed up and adapted, reflecting that this attention was going to be okay. Since no one had met the baby, he was being passed around with a lot of fanfare. A few tears flowed, but he too eventually warmed up to all of these strangers.

Casual conversation eventually settled into its usual rhythm. Mother and Grandma Nanny settled themselves into what everyone called the piano room where there would be less commotion and noise. This room served multiple purposes, such as an extra sitting room, bedroom when needed, but mostly it housed the piano.

This piano had been a gift to my Mother from her father when she was in her early twenties and had been a part of her life ever since. Playing this piano had become a solace to her when she needed to have some relief from the stresses in her life. It also was a source for her personal entertainment and an expression of who she was. She loved her gospel music, singing of her hope in her risen savior, Jesus Christ.

Grandpa Garfield was like the pied piper as he loved children and they all knew it. He loved being with them. He was drawn to their impish ways and with his outgoing personality he was always a hit. Children loved his teasing ways. When Grandpa Garfield was around, the children would always be close by. He had a gift for becoming childlike relating to the younger set with great appeal.

Everyone knows that babies have their needs which demand immediate attention. Our baby was hungry and needed his bottle. With Grandpa Garfield's natural love for children he instantly volunteered to feed his new great grandson his bottle. Relinquishing that responsibility was a no brainer. Sitting them both down in the old knitter's rocker with a bottle in hand they could now enjoy this moment together. I went on with other activities, but before it was too late the following scene caught my eye. It has seared itself into my memory and I have never been able to let it go.

I ignored this memory placing it in the, "I'll do something later with this thought," category. However, this scene kept returning to my mind, and again I would place it on my someday to do list. Eventually this scene began to haunt me in ways that I could no longer ignore. The emotions which had been emanated from that moment had become something that scratched my brain for attention, like a cat and its scratching post.

I came to the conclusion I could no longer ignore my thoughts. My memory of this scene had so etched itself into my inner soul it was now impossible to ignore what I had witnessed. What happened that day has passed through my consciousness many times over. One day I sat down and penned the following poem hoping to show its simplicity yet capture the richness of an extraordinary event and the depth of its lesson that came in unexpected ways, from unexpected places, in unpredicted times.

The Well Worn Rocker

There stood a well worn rocker
In the middle of a lived in room
Much greater issues were at stake
Memories and new beginnings to contemplate.
A weathered face, a body bent, a mind
That drifted to a time of the past
Wondering how the years had gone so fast.
Now he would cherish the moment that he had
To love and to hold this new little lad.
This bright eyed baby with skin of silk

Silent Tears

Who was cherishing his bottle of milk.
One so very young, the other so very old
This time spent together, more precious than gold.
Time almost gone, yet just beginning
Two different lives, yet were sharing
This moment in time, that God had planned
Two generations, one starting, the other soon to end
A great-grandson, and a great grandfather
Just for a moment, shared this well worn rocker.

Baby: John Robert Stroebel born on September 28, 1964
Great Grandpa Garfield Thompson: Passed away February 6, 1966 at age 87. In
July 1966, he would have been 88
Family visit in the summer of 1965

Sacred Moments

THE POWER THESE MOMENTS EXUDED hammered the reality that one life was fading fast and the other life was just beginning. The solitude the two shared would never come again and could never be replaced. Oblivious to the world around them, sharing this time together was truly sacred. Grandpa Garfield was lost in his world of thoughts and our baby was completely focused on his warm bottle of milk while being held in the attentive arms of his great grandfather whom he would never get to know.

As Grandpa Garfield slowly rocked his great grandson in this knitter's rocker, I could see him studying this little stranger of his own blood. I tried to be inconspicuous as I watched this scene unfold. Grandpa G studied his skin, the shape of his body, and other physical characteristics as he cradled this infant in his arms. He listened to the rhythm of his breathing and the sounds of nursing a bottle.

Grandpa knew in his heart what he really thought. I could read the reflective emotions in his face. He would never be able to be a part of his own blood's future. He would love to be able to take his great grandchild fishing as that was one of his personal passions. He knew that would never be. However, this rocker had provided a shared meeting place especially for the two of them.

This rocker was not only cradling two human beings but also cradling a big question, as well as performing a dual mission. It was witnessing a fading flame and at the same time ushering in the unfolding future of the other. "How can the one living in the future know of the past and not have it be lost and yet understand that the one who lived in the past will never know the future?" This question begged for an answer, gnawing at my mind to keep me from ignoring it. This was a haunting question that would not leave no matter how hard I have tried ignoring these reoccurring thoughts.

This rocker scene was simple and routine, which occurs in every family at one time or another. There was nothing extraordinary about it, except, this time the extraordinary seemed to define it.

As we always did after our Canadian family visit we would return to our life in Milwaukee. A few months later we received a call that Grandpa Garfield had passed away from a heart attack. "Life is like a mist, it appears for a little time and then is gone." James 4:14

We were all saddened by the news of Grandpa Garfield's passing. The effort we were making to maintain family connections meant more now as we mourned for him. We would miss him on our visits. The children would no longer experience his playful ways which was sad to think about.

The memory of our infant son being embraced in such a way by his great grandfather resurfaced again and again. How would our children know their heritage? How would they learn of the legacies left by those who had lived before them? Professional legacies are often talked about and many times praised, but what about the spiritual and character legacies? Were they not important too, maybe even more important.

Without my husband's cooperation, this effort to maintain family connections would never have reached the level it had. I respected his efforts to maintain these family connections and be consistent in those efforts as well. The memories which our immediate family was developing were invaluable to us. Continuing in these efforts was a given.

Some other thoughts began to enter my mind raising questions that dogged my brain looking for some direction to my thinking.

Is it possible the orchestrating of the intersection of these two lives which happened in the blink of an eye began decades, or even a century ago, or perhaps even a longer period of time in the past? God has promised to walk before us preparing our path to bring about His purposes. Destiny is a predetermined path which we have not had any conscious personal input to bring about events. Often, we credit Divine Intervention to bring a sense of meaning into circumstances that we don't understand, when we had no part in orchestrating such happenings. We hear comments like, "It was meant to be." Mankind also tends to refer to such events as a coincidence, eliminating any concept of Divine Influence.

A mind stretching thought has been articulated. When God created the world which we experience, He looked down through the ages and visualized every baby that would be born, knowing their birth date and the day in which their life would end. To be able to grasp the immensity of that thought, one has to be able to grasp the vastness of the omnipotence, omnipresence, and omniscience of God. Those three characteristics of God really bend the mind when in search of spiritual principles that relate to our everyday lives.

Was this blink of an eye event meant to provide an impetus for sharing and recording a family history? To share a legacy of faith by family members who have experienced tough times and yet tell a parallel story of a never ending mystery? And in the end discovering answers and finding victory when hope had been so elusive? Emotional conflict would spin around in my mind for a long time regarding this matter. Three short words showed up in unrelated events that happened within a short period of time, giving the same message. "Just Do It." I asked myself, "Are these words more of God whispers in my life?"

A presentation from a well-known speaker climaxed my thinking in making that final commitment to finish this memoir. Lessons learned from the life of Nehemiah who was building that huge wall, were confrontational. Having started this project of writing, but being double minded, staying focused, and resisting distractions was a lesson emphatically emphasized. Another lesson gleaned was stay firm in what you believe and don't lose heart. I had been doubled minded about believing in a purpose for my writing. The last lesson learned which penetrated my mind was, "Finish What You Start," and "Don't Become Discouraged." That was like stubbing my toe on a stone. Since I had already started, but had allowed a lot of distractions, I interpreted it as a command not to be ignored. Instead of this being a God whisper it felt more like a shout in my ear. Every point made by the speaker was practical and seemingly related to my mind set in that moment, providing me with a real sense of purpose for continuing.

"Just Start in the Beginning and Write What Comes to Your Mind," were some directional thoughts. Had these been God whispers giving me direction when I wasn't sure how to proceed? I was reviewing these thoughts again in my mind after hearing this speaker's presentation. The most emphatic thought again reoccurred. Just Do It And Don't Allow Any More Distractions. Take Your Writing Project To The Finish Line. "Have not I commanded you to be strong and courageous, don't be terrified nor be discouraged for the Lord your God is with you wherever you go." Joshua 1:9 As a result of this promise I have felt His presence and guidance.

Writing this memoir was now also expanding to a broader horizon than I had originally envisioned. The urgency of recording the history of my Grandparents through stories shared by my mother seemed to become of utter importance. I could not let their story be lost and forgotten. These stories were too rich to be allowed to fade away into insignificance, especially after witnessing the rocker scene.

My own emotional health had greatly improved during our early years of family trips; however, I still needed to come to terms with my mother's emotional unhappiness and the mystery surrounding my father. I was in need of a lot more answers to my questions, however, elusiveness remained

Promises of a New World

THE ROCKER SCENE had so impacted my spirit and penetrated me to the core of my being. Portraying my grandparent's personalities and the qualities of whom they had become seemed way too important to allow their legacies to become dust in the fading past. Their lives could not be contained within the limitations of an obituary column. A life lived deserves more than a single column printed in the local newspaper.

My grandparent's story is not only part of my own families' history but their lives were also affected by historical and personal events beyond their control. Events shaped their lives for years to come and those of their descendents. Their influence still hovers over me like ray of sunshine, pushing me to hold dear some of the admirable qualities they seemed to innately possess. Some characteristics were gained through the fire of life which requires me to offer my deepest respect and affection. Their lives also challenge my own perseverance during tough times. I doubt the idea of a personal legacy ever crossed their minds or that one day their granddaughter would present to the world snippets of their personal lives sharing their triumphs and defeats.

Since I have to go back in time to properly lay the foundation of their lives, I will begin with "There Were Rumors of a New World."

Western Canada was a sparsely populated land until the late eighteen hundreds. Prior to this time, the native Blackfoot Indians, the Stony Indians, and the Athabasca Nation had occupied the territory. Few immigrants had made their way to this new country. The Canadian government was making an effort to increase the population in order to spur its development as a nation.

The Canadian Pacific Railway helped to create settlements through the southern sections of the Canadian Prairies. The Canadian National Railway developed the northern route. It was during the 1880"s that the east coast and the western provinces were connected to each other. The rail system did not reach the west coast until the 1960's, then fully connecting the east with the west. The railway systems had a huge impact on Canada's development as it also did in the United States.

The influx of new immigrants started in the mid 1890's, ending with the beginning of WWI. Advertising of free land by the Canadian government created a rush of new immigrants.

The Homestead Act was not unlike the Homestead Act of the United States government for developing the central prairie states in the mid 1860's to 1870's. In both cases the purposes of the governments were to develop the sparsely populated states or provinces.

Free land was given to you provided you made the specified improvements within a specified time. Following these specifications would allow you to make a land claim for a title to be issued from the Canadian government.

Americans from many states responded to these promises of free land in the "New World." After the civil war the southern United States economy was in an especially depressive condition. Due to these New World promises my maternal grandparents responded to the Canadian government's advertising. They were a young married couple from North Carolina with a nine month old baby, my mother.

This advertising of free land was also great news to the land hungry Europeans.

The idea of going to a "New World" held the hope of a future with the promise of a better life than what they were experiencing. For many in Europe, land ownership was limited to a few acres if they were lucky.

Others were kept in servants roles with land ownership impossible. To own land was only a dream that could exist in their minds. Making a new life for themselves by their own determination and hard work, held great promise. This advertising of free land through Europe, Scandinavia, and England, proved to be a fruitful endeavor by the Canadians. My paternal grandparents were some of those immigrants who made their way from England.

Some immigrants came through the indentured servant system, agreeing to serve the one who paid their expenses for an agreed upon time. Wealthier immigrants were willing to embark on a new adventure in order to take advantage of opportunities to add to their wealth. Lawbreakers were also part of that list that came to these new lands. Escaping from the local law was their chance to start a new life joining the influx of new immigrants having their own influence.

Regardless of who the immigrants were, personal possessions were packed away in sturdy trunks being made ready for shipping by either ocean craft or through the railway system. Trunks had to be solidly constructed to withstand the rough conditions.

Contents would include winter clothing, linens, religious symbols, garden seeds, onions, garlic, potatoes for food and seed, and perhaps a few keepsakes if there was room in the trunk. Farming and carpentry tools would also be included for shipping. Tools would be the life blood of survival in the new world.

The Nebraska museum called, "The Gateway To The West" located on interstate 80, has a posted plaque which reads:

> "The Cowards Never Started
> The Weak Died On the Way
> Only the Strong Arrived
> They Were the Pioneers"

Only the owner of the heart upon departure understands the depth of emotion involved when such life changing decisions are made. Leaving the known for the unknown breeds excitement, then anxiety, remembering that hardships were certain to be lurking around unknown corners. Perhaps there was a lot of personal denial in their thinking, believing that survival would be the winner and any defeat would be a stranger. However, desperation was a motivating factor in considering theses life changing adventures.

Cultural changes would be drastic. Leaving those you know and love, facing the fact that in all probability you will never see the left behind family again. They would believe that their "Goodbyes" were final ones. "See You Later," would no longer be a part of their daily language.

Communication after departure was almost nonexistent. Mail delivery would take a lot longer than the snail mail we are familiar with in our present day. Often it would take a year or more to hear from each other, if there was communication that took place at all.

However, the desire for adventure drives one to do the extraordinary. That is the reason we have men who have developed aircraft, spaceships, traveling to the moon, mountain climbers who have conquered Mt Everest, war time heroes, and all who have not valued their lives more than the reward of adventure and success. God has gifted minds that have made tremendous contributions in the fields of science, medicine, and industrial inventions, that have benefited mankind beyond measure. They are the ones of whom we call the movers and shakers of our world. These adventure minded intellects don't let fear be an obstacle, but something to be conquered and managed.

My family's ancestors were on that list of those who were determined, persevered, and were patient. These were characteristics that were needed in generous amounts to succeed in their effort to fulfill their dreams and provide a better future for their families.

Leaving Europe and setting sail to Canada, their arrival port was Halifax, Nova Scotia. After their arrival, the trek west was made possible by the railway systems.

Wherever the railway set up a station, a new settlement would develop. These early residential structures were primitively built wooden or sod shack, with dirt floors. Of course, in time these primitive conditions were replaced, progressing to more comfortable dwellings.

Grasslands where the buffalo roamed eventually became cultivated and planted grain fields. The cold and cool climates were conducive to growing a variety of grains but too far north for corn production. As grain production increased, grain elevators were built along the rail system, enabling the ease of shipping. These iconic tall angular structures had lots of storage space. Eventually, the farmer could haul his harvest directly to the elevator, keeping only in reserve what he needed for current use, such as feeding his livestock or storing seed for next year's replanting. Freight trains were able to pull right into elevators, stopping under large chutes for ease of loading. It took time for primitive beginnings to progress into this more convenient system. It naturally was a process of progression that took place over many decades. The grain production from the prairie provinces eventually became part of the bread basket of the world.

This harvesting system provided a ready market for the farmer. When he took his grain to the elevator it was immediately weighed, a price per bushel was established on the spot, and he could then look forward to a paycheck which would soon follow. Because harvest only happened once a year a farmer could look forward to a paycheck only once a year. In today's culture that is hard to fathom as we live and function on a weekly or monthly basis.

The flat prairie fields made it possible for these tall angular wooden structures to become landmarks, visible for miles on the horizon. These elevators and the train stations gave a reason for hamlets to exist. They were the early beginnings of community life. These original hamlets have grown into modern communities and the large cities of today.

Pre 1890, Winnipeg became the most populated city of the West. Regina became known as the Queen City of the plains named after a town in England. Saskatoon was a railroad station settlement. Calgary, with only a few thousand, was a primitive cow town with smelly dusty streets, horse drawn buggies, and wagons. Maybe there the fresh mountain air didn't always smell very fresh. Edmonton became known as a trading post. Vancouver, being on the pacific coast, was a sea port.

British Columbia was very different from the flat prairie provinces where you could see miles and miles in the distance with those iconic grain elevators on the far distant horizon. It is a province with its own special flavor. Mountains with high peaks, valleys, lakes, rivers, with heavily forested landscapes, exist all the way from its eastern border to its western boundary on the Pacific creating a lot of variety to its topography. This province has some of the most exquisite scenery in the world. It provides a feast of vistas for the eyes to behold. British Columbia has been known for its wood products industry and still is. With its vast forest lands, it is a major provider of this industry.

Social class and style was not very much a part of the homesteading mindset. They were practical, physically and mentally hardy, and very independent. Survival was their goal. During those days I can well imagine that in New York City the social class that you were in would be influenced by the breed of the horse you drove and the style of the buggy or carriage you chose to own, giving you prestigious transportation. In the developing country sides, the thought of any old horse will do as long as it can walk and pull something. If there was no horse, then a donkey or a mule. As for the buggy or wagon, the bare necessities were inspected and needed. The wheels, frame, box and tongue, had to be sound. Function was important.

Heading North to Alberta

ALBERTA WAS THE PROVINCE that my maternal grandparents chose to make their homestead claim. The reasons why they chose Alberta were never revealed to me nor did it ever come up in conversation. Alberta just seemed to be the place that they came to seek a future, and that was all.

I do know that historical and extraordinary personal events became life directing influences in their early lives. How much an influence is based on my own reflection of conversations which I witnessed and comments made during casual conversation at family gatherings.

Both of my maternal grandparents were from North Carolina and born soon after the Civil War ended. Grandpa Garfield was born 1878 and Grandma Nanny in 1882. The economy of North Carolina along with the rest of the southern United States was in a depressive state after the Civil War and struggling with no recovery in sight for some time. With the advertising of free land no doubt there became a huge personal draw to head north to Alberta. Knowing my grandfather, taking advantage of the Canadian government's offer would not only be an adventure, but also an economic answer for him and his small family.

Prior to their heading north, personal events had a great influence in their decision making process. Without these personal experiences their tale would probably read much differently.

Grandpa Garfield was the eldest son of a North Carolina country medical doctor, who rode around the country side on horseback making his house calls to treat his patients. (Presently, the general hospital in Sparta, North Carolina, has a large plaque honoring his father, Dr Robert Thompson, for his early medical contribution to their community.) Grandpa Garfield had planned to follow in his father's footsteps. He wanted to study medicine at the same Texas medical school where his father had graduated. His goal was to finish his first level of education then apply for medical school. That being completed he proceeded to apply. Along with the application he was to send the results of a physical and of course, he was expecting everything to go well. He had always been an excellent student not anticipating that anything would be hindering him from pursuing his goals.

Unfortunately, Grandpa Garfield was in for a huge disappointment. His physical results revealed that he was infected with tuberculosis. This called for an immediate change of plans. Instead of pursuing his medical education, his own physical survival was now at stake.

The usual treatment for tuberculosis was a lengthy two year isolation stay in a sanitarium. Grandpa G was gregarious and isolation for him would have been a nightmare. Fortunately for him with a medical person in the family, his father recommended an entirely different kind of treatment, one that was very uncommon, and for that matter maybe never heard of before.

Out of this discussion between father and son, an unusual idea for a treatment evolved. Father instructed his son to leave North Carolina, go to Montana and get a sheepherding job. Montana had a dry, cold climate compared to North Carolina with its heat and humidity. Dr. Thompson instructed him to sleep outside every night and to not spend one single night indoors, even in the winter.

Off to Montana Grandpa Garfield went, doing everything medically which his father had instructed. He got his sheepherding job and slept outdoors for two full years, even in the winter. I shiver every time I think about that Montana winter. Deep snow and bone chilling winds with subzero temperatures don't bring to mind any cozy or warm fuzzy feelings, especially when that is the state of your bedroom as well. Only his determination and perseverance helped him recover from this infectious disease.

Selma J. Stroebel

Recovery from this dreadful disease was his goal. But, my mind wonders off to what he must have endured during those two years in Montana trying to survive those severe winter days. Growing up in Alberta, I know from personal experience how quickly and drastically the North Pole winds can change the temperatures of the day. Temps can go from a spring-like sunny day and melting snow to clouds and a winter blizzard in a matter of hours with subzero temperatures. Being prepared for winter drama is a science in itself. It is a must to be weather aware for your life can be in danger if you are not.

The only equipment that I became aware of, as I listened to a few comments, was his mummy like sleeping bag that completely enshrouded his body by its canvas and down. If he had used any other survival equipment, I do not know. There was never any mention of it. I can't imagine that sleeping bag being the only piece of equipment that he used to survive those Montana winters with any kind of comfort.

Survival equipment had not evolved into the science that it has today. Survival techniques in that era would be made up by your own instincts and resourcefulness. He never parted with that down sleeping bag. It accompanied him on his mountain hunting trips, even when he was up into his seventies. Grandpa was a hardy soul who certainly didn't cringe when faced with a challenge. Without that personality trait, his recovery from tuberculosis probably would read very differently. The length of time that he spent in Montana would have been approximately the same length of time he would have spent in the sanitarium. After this rigorous experience in Montana, he returned to North Carolina, his father's solution being successful and his health renewed.

He did not pursue medical school again. Why the direction of his life took a different turn, reasons were never stated. However, influences that abounded and were spoken of often along with personality traits, seemed to be the ingredients which empowered the decision making process in setting a family life direction.

Silent Tears

The economy in the South remained in a depressive state, still being affected by the Civil War, even though much time had passed. Opportunities for a young man to provide for a family were limited. It was during this phase of my grandfather's life that the advertising by Canada attracted homesteaders west to populate and develop the country. This seemed to be the opportunity that he was looking for. He had already experienced the harshness of a northern climate and survived, so that was not a threat. Through this extended rugged outdoor living experience in Montana, he had developed a strong spirit of independence. Along with that independent spirit emerged an adventurous drive, a powerful combination. He had also developed a love of nature and the outdoor lifestyle, becoming a part of him that lasted a lifetime.

Life was changing for Grandpa Garfield. During this transition period of his life he met and married my grandmother, Nanny Edna Abshire from Laurel Springs, North Carolina. She lived only a short distance away from his home town of Sparta. The time period was just after the turn of the twentieth century. They were married September 29, 1904.

Montana and Alberta share a lot of similarity. I suspect that influenced my grandparents' choice of geographic location. This western state and province are bordered by the Rocky Mountains on their western edge. Both have beautiful mountain vistas, rolling foothills, prairie land, ranching and farming, along with the prospect of excellent hunting opportunities. The prospect of free land and all of these similarities, I suspect, were the prodding forces that stirred Grandpa's inner call. Especially since he had already experienced those similarities, while recovering from his illness.

Possessions were gathered together and packed into sturdy trunks. Grandma gathered together some of their wedding gifts. Her few linens and china were limited but were some of her favorite take along items. Practical clothing and her big hats, of which she was known for, were not eliminated. She had a reputation for wearing large stylish hats and that was something that she was not going to leave behind.

Grandpa took charge of packing the tools. His axes and hand saws would be very necessary for clearing land that would all be done manually. Livestock also became part of the cargo. He had obtained a couple of horses and a cow that were to be included with the tools and personal items all of which were to be shipped by rail to their new destination. How they managed to transport all of these possessions from the rail-yard to their homestead is a feat I was never privy to nor do I remember comments being made concerning this leg of their trip.

In the early spring of 1906, they, too, said their goodbyes like all the other immigrants before them had done. They, too, experienced the loneliness of heart and homesickness before they departed. Not knowing whether you would ever see family again and those familiar family faces created deep emotional moments. Family traditions would also in time become a distant memory. Private thoughts would again question the decision that had already been made, while the whys would come forward to confirm the reasons for their commitment to this unknown future.

Grandpa Garfield had been much more emotionally prepared for this kind of adventure. His time spent in Montana herding sheep and dealing with his illness had already prepared him to a large degree. Also, Grandpa had an inborn independent nature which had sprouted deep roots through his rugged days of outdoor living on that Montana sheep ranch.

Grandma Nanny had not gone through such emotional preparedness. However, she apparently determined to persevere and endure the unknown with her baby and husband. There was a lot of homesickness on her part, which I absorbed through comments my mother made.

Upon boarding the train bound for the Alberta Montana border, Grandpa G was 27 years old. Grandma Nanny was four years younger, being 23 years old. Their baby girl, Virginia Edna, my mother, was nine months old. This was a real soul searching and challenging trip for a young family to make under such circumstances.

Life on the Homestead

JULY 1, 1865- CANADA officially became a Dominion under the flag of England, the Union Jack. This land was a new frontier, open to the world to come and start a new life.

Respondents to the land offers were many, since advertising to populate this sparsely populated country had gone out to Europe, England and the United States. This mix of nationalities provided an interesting mixture of people from many nations in the developing communities. Neighbors were also a mix of nations. Neighbors were really important to this new life, as they made up a support system when someone needed help, or simply a friend.

Beginning life on a homestead provides a story all of its own. How Grandpa Garfield and Grandma Nanny decided upon this plot of land, I do not know. Family conversations never alluded to that decision. I only know that they found a plot of land out in the sticks of west central Alberta, closer to the western mountain region than the eastern prairie landscapes. When I refer to sticks, I mean it was isolated and covered with trees with few neighbors. This was a virgin plot meaning that it had never been privately owned but was government property.

To own this land and have it become their own, making improvements was part of the deal. The homesteader had to clear thirty acres and live on the land for at least six months of the year. Cultivating, building, and fencing, had to be done within a three year period or he would lose his ten dollar bet with the government. If the conditions were met, he would receive a "Certificate of Recommendation for Homestead Patent" from the Department of the Interior.

This plot of land which they chose was twenty five miles from the nearest bare necessity store or the once in a while mail delivery post office. Getting to either one was a two day trip on horseback.

Getting to this land involved following trails over the hills and valleys along with crossing a couple of rivers. The rivers had similar names. One the Little Red Deer River and the other was The Big Red Deer River, later often referred to as Little Red and Big Red. These trails eventually evolved into primitive roads.

These wagon wheel rutted roads were almost impassable when the frost left the ground in the spring. Deep mud holes would form from wagon traffic and melting snow. Early fall and winter snows made movement in the winter difficult. Horseback and horse-drawn sleighs or wagons were the basic mode of transportation. In the deep snow and the spring season mud-holes, the early cars just got stuck because they were unable to navigate through such conditions. Horses were a very valuable possession.

Life would definitely not be comparable to today's fast lane, but in reality painfully slow to us as we think about life back then. However, living a slow life to them was normal with little expectation of it changing much. Survival was the immediate goal. Hardships and challenges were expected and perseverance was the determining factor in their survival. Giving up was not a part of their thinking.

Their first abode was very primitive. Grandpa Garfield managed to cut down enough logs to build a one room log shack before that first winter set in. It had a dirt floor with a sod roof, which I can imagine leaked like a sieve when there was melting snow or rain. The doorway was a real winner. A wool blanket was hung over the door to keep the cold out. I can't imagine that blanket keeping out much more than a few snowflakes. I can well imagine Grandma kept asking herself "What in the world have

I gotten myself into?" How they survived that cold Alberta winter with a young baby is beyond my comprehension to grasp the full extent of what they faced and endured. In my mind, they also spent a lot of time shivering and were very cold much of the time.

Fortunately, wood was plentiful providing plenty of fuel for heat. Also Grandpa never became known for his carpentry skills, even later in life. That was never his gift.

I never heard my grandparents talk much about their homestead years. It was my mother that related these life experiences to me as she recalled them. After all, their story became her story as well. She and her brother had lived through those homestead years with their parents and had experienced the victories and defeats firsthand. For my mother and her brother experiencing the rugged life in their early years were character building events which also produced hardy and strong willed individuals.

My mother was a storyteller. She remembered details of events that were important to her whether she had personally experienced them or whether it was a story retold to her. This is one that was retold to her as she would have been too young to remember. It is short but has its punch.

Her father had seen the need for extra muscle power for this homesteading adventure. He knew he would need horses for clearing the land, tilling the soil for either a garden spot or for a grain field. He had selected a couple of horses which he felt would meet these imagined needs. He had them shipped along with their other goods during the initial trip by rail from North Carolina to Alberta. All went well, until shortly after they arrived at their selected land plot. The horses became ill and it was determined that they had contracted a disease called strangles. Today there may be a different name for it and a treatment available; however, the verdict for them was that their horses had to be destroyed. Their land was put under two-year quarantine.

During the shipping, a stop was made at the border between the United States and Canada for veterinary inspection. At the border, animals being shipped were not kept isolated from each other. After a mental review of their trip, it was concluded that the border crossing was where his horses had contracted the fatal disease. This was a huge loss for them and a devastating blow at the very beginning of their homesteading journey. All I know of this story is that my grandparents did not give up, but stayed on with determination using what they had for tools; his axe, handsaw, and shovel.

Neighbors would gather together to help dig wells for a water supply. Apparently on this plot of land the water table was not that far down. Neighbors would also help each other whenever a construction project would be undertaken. A lot of camaraderie between neighbors was common. My grandparents discovered that one of their neighbors was from North Carolina as well. A close bond developed between the two couples.

 A garden was a must. Seeds that had been packed in their trunks provided some vegetables for the makeshift kitchen table. Carrots, peas, beans, and potatoes grow well in cool summer climates. These became a staple. After each season, seeds would be kept from the harvest for replanting in the following year.

 Wild berries provided a nutritional supplement to their diet. Blueberries and highland cranberries grew wild in the woods, so if you wanted some, a berry search would become an expedition for the day. Jack Pines were a signal that blueberries might be near if a late frost hadn't killed the blossoms. It seemed that Jack Pines and wild blueberries grew near each other. Highland cranberries would also come into season close to the same time as the blueberries. These berries were a highly nutritious wild fruit.

 These wild berries became a delicacy to us all in time. We became very fond of their flavor. Grandma Nanny would can them by the half-gallon jar. I learned many years later that these highland cranberries were the same berries that in Norway are called ling-on-berries. They flourish in the colder climates and higher altitudes which Alberta and Norway have in common.

Another similarity between the two geographical locations is the very long daylight hours during the short summer growing season. However, during those first years of homesteading, berries provided a nutritional fruit to the diet when other fruits were not available.

Another nutritional source, were the wild prairie roses that grew almost everywhere providing rose hips that could be consumed in tea. The rumor was that if you consumed rose hips you would not get the flu. Today we know that they are rich in vitamin C. The wild prairie rose also became the official provincial flower.

During those early first years, the preservation of food for the winter was a problem. To keep vegetables from freezing they were buried in freshly dug holes which were then covered with leaves or straw to keep the ground from freezing over the vegetables. Fresh meat was packed in salt for short term preserving until the canning method could be utilized.

Their meat source was mainly wildlife. Grandpa Garfield loved to hunt. Venison, moose, and elk were the big game meat suppliers. Fill-ins were rabbits, squirrels, and pheasants. Without the ready supply of wild meat, survival would have been questionable for the homesteaders. In fact, when the berries were gone and the vegetables were all consumed meat was all they had until a new season appeared on the calendar. Warm weather for gardens to produce again would be months away. Mother mentioned how much they missed fresh fruit and vegetables, stating her palate yearned for them.

Trunks didn't hold many kitchen supplies. It took time to get a cook stove and canning jars to preserve food. My Grandmother stocked her kitchen from estate sales. Circumstances would dictate that some homesteaders would have to give up their pioneer lifestyle. The accumulation of basic kitchen equipment took time to accumulate. Frugality was a word that had immense meaning.

In time, the accumulation of homegrown chickens took place, providing another meat supply as well as a supply of fresh eggs.

Mother related to us that Grandpa used the usual method of off with the head over a chopping block, whenever they wanted chicken for dinner. However, whenever Grandpa wasn't available for this kind of job Grandma had her own method. Apparently Grandma became a reflection of Annie Oakley when using her gun skills, having been forced to learn and found them to be necessary at times. Apparently, she became a pretty good shot being skilled enough to shoot a chicken in the head with accuracy. The head is not a very large target. Albeit, I guess you do what you got to do, if you want to eat.

Having to perform this kind of task, would have been a real cultural shock for a lady that liked to be a stylish dresser and wear large fashionable hats. In this setting she was a long way from North Carolina.

Grandpa Garfield was also a storyteller. Storytelling seems to run in the family. The following happens to be about a personal event which included reading his own obituary.

He needed to make the long arduous twenty five mile horseback ride to the store and post office. This was one way so that meant a fifty mile round trip. This equestrian trip was not something which he was unfamiliar with as he had made this trip before, knew what to expect along the way, and approximately how much time would be involved. Sometimes riders would stay in a hotel overnight before making the return journey; however, many times the travel would be completed in a single day. The pioneer horse really received a work out.

This time his seemingly routine trip was different. The two year quarantine on their homestead had been lifted making it possible for him to replace his destroyed saddle horse.

Big Red's water was elevated due to spring rains and melting glaciers in the mountains. A quick flowing body of water due to its elevated sources made this river a stream to be wary of. However, to get to services it had to be forded and there was no way around it since it flowed between their homestead and the small community services. On this trip, determination to get services clouded Grandpa's judgment. The out- come could have been disastrous.

Saddling up his ride and heading down the trail, coming to the river's edge he urged his horse forward into the fast flowing water. The water became deeper than anticipated causing the horse to swim and at the same time moving them both downstream. The force of the water caused his saddle to turn to the horse's off side washing Grandpa out of his seat. Being able to grab the horse's tail as he swam by, they were both able to make it the river's edge sopping wet but missing his hat. Noticing his hat floating down stream but irretrievable, he remounted his horse and continued on.

In the meantime, a friend was downstream fishing in a Big Red tributary, noticed a hat floating by and recognizing the hat as belonging to a friend became alarmed. This friend went upstream to investigate and found nothing, coming to the conclusion that his friend had drowned in this cold glacier and spring-fed river. He went to the RCMP to report this seeming loss of his friend, and again the conclusion was made that Grandpa had drowned in the high water.

His obituary was published in the local newspaper. When it became known that he had survived, Grandpa was given a copy of his own obituary.

Grandpa had another story that he liked to tell. This story was a reflection of another aspect of homestead life, and that of personal hygiene. Grandpa was so fastidious about personal care, he found this story to be very humorous.

There was this middle-aged lady of the community, who like many others, out of necessity lived the primitive lifestyle of the homesteader. She apparently had a severe case of arthritis in one of her knees. It had been bothering her for quite some time. Finally, she decided to go and visit the doctor hoping to get some relief from her pain. During the examination the doctor asked her to lift her skirt so that he could examine her knee. When she did lift her skirt, the doctor exclaimed, "Oh my, your knee is dirty!" Her reply was, "Well, doctor this is the one I washed."

Whether this story had any truth or not, it did reflect the difficulty some had in their personal care during those basic survival years. In reality, it is a believable story, after learning about those early living conditions. However, it was a story Grandpa enjoyed telling.

Those homesteading years offered other challenges as well. Roads were not really roads but trails developing into more passable trails as the population grew. Getting around during the spring when the frost was coming out of the ground, roads would be nothing more than muddy wagon ruts. Massive mud holes where melting snow and spring rain water would gather could make those areas impassible with any kind of primitive auto. Horseback riders didn't have a problem getting around as a horse could go anywhere. Horse drawn wagons were immediate solutions if drawn by heavy draft horses.

Winter time posed different conditions for getting around. Deep winter snows and storms along with extremely cold temperatures were other obstacles. Horseback was always the reliable method. Wagons would be refitted with sleigh runners instead of wagon wheels for winter transportation, again drawn by the draft horse. Community snow removal had not come into vogue. Everyone was on their own for getting off their land during such times, and that was not often.

The breed of horse you rode or drove was not important. Any old horse or wagon would do. Style or design was not a quality that anyone looked for, since function that could meet needs of those first land dwellers, was of the utmost importance. Bare necessities and reliability were the demanding qualities that were needed for life to proceed with any sense of progress.

This lifestyle was a far cry from developed towns and cities where the well-bred horse you owned and the Cadillac quality of the carriages which carried you, offered community prestige. A young gentleman with a well-bred horse and a fancy buggy could make many heads turn. The contrast between the polished class of the more elite in society, and the unpolished homesteader could not be more stark, as in any time period of history. With the invention and advancements of the auto and the street car, this industrial progress changed everything.

Immigrants were practical, independent, hard working, resourceful, and not used to life being convenient.

My maternal grandparents lived on the homestead for eight years, before circumstances beyond their control entered their lives.

A New Direction

MY GRANDPARENTS SURVIVED those early pioneer days and managed to adjust to this rugged life. They learned a lot about what it takes to develop their land and home. Farming, hunting, and gardening in this northern climate had been a real education. Hard work was at the core of everything that spelled progress and change. Those severely cold northern winters were something that had to be reckoned with in advance or you didn't survive.

The lack of physical comforts presented hardships as well. Just trying to keep warm in the winter was difficult. Cooking, bathing, and laundry, were challenges with a limited water supply. All water had to be carried in a bucket. With no indoor plumbing, a trip to the outhouse in forty degrees below zero weather was a trip to remember. These were daily challenges to be met.

Both of my grandparents were gregarious. They had met and made friends with their neighbors and others in similar states of progress. Grandma had made the adjustment from the USA, southern country, to a whole different kind of country, which was of course the pioneer type. She survived the shock of the cultural change from wearing her big hats which she was known for, to her plain utilitarian attire toting her gun and hoe. Life was moving forward in the slow lane, as we would say today, but it was moving forward. When their second child was born, (my uncle), they returned to North Carolina for his birth. After their son's birth, a return to the homestead was made and life seemed to continue to stabilize for them.

However, unexpected events have a way of interrupting our plans declaring in an unmistakable manner that life will never be the same. Historical and personal events stepped in to dramatically change the direction of their lives at a time when they felt that the direction was already set. Adjustments were being made, progress seemed to be occurring, a future was being planned for, and the reality of its fruition produced hope.

World War I had become a hot topic of their day with continual dismal news. Canadians were volunteering for Canadian military service and Grandpa Garfield decided to become one of their number, after giving it a lot of thought.

Each volunteer was required to have a medical checkup before enlisting in the service. Grandpa went like all of the others for his physical. When it was completed, the doctor informed him of his real condition. The war would be over before they would take men like him. He was told that his heart was in bad shape and he would never see the age of forty. He suggested that Grandpa go home and get his house in order. His future was short. He was thirty five years old and grandma was thirty one.

My mother recalls a soberness existing in the air that evening after her father's medical report. She remembers that both she and her brother were sent to bed early. As children will do, their curiosity reigns over obedience to authority. She remembers eavesdropping on the low whispering of her parents' discussing the disturbing news. Apparently, her father admitted, that even before the doctor's report he had found it difficult to do the hard physical labor. He had not said anything, keeping his thoughts to himself. I don't know how he rationalized serving in the military knowing how he had been feeling.

The reality of a necessary change stared them in the face. They were feeling like they were experiencing an unwanted intruder who had just arrived.

The needed change took root in Grandpa's mind. Within a year he returned to the United States with the purpose of looking for employment.

Grandma and the children moved to the nearest town, Olds, Alberta, renting a house and waiting for word from their father and husband. They waited another year before returning to Sparta, North Carolina. They left the homestead never to return.

Upon returning to North Carolina, Grandma Nanny became very ill. It was determined that as a result of using and drinking contaminated well water during their stay in the rental house, she had contracted typhoid fever. She became so seriously ill that the family was expecting death almost anytime. Suddenly a glimpse of hope in her condition became evident. As her health began to improve, arrangements for the children's future was put on hold.

I never learned about the length of her recovery. I do know she had some negative side effects as a result of a metabolic imbalance caused by her illness. She experienced severe weight gain, which lasted for an extended period of time. Grandma was about five foot five inches and became close to weighing two hundred pounds. In time she did come back to her normal weight. Apparently her body was eventually able to metabolically balance and stabilize itself. This was 1916. She and the children remained in the household of Grandpa's family for two years.

In the meantime, Grandpa Garfield was able to get a representative position with a pharmaceutical company headquartered in St Louis, Missouri. He would be selling pharmaceutical supplies to hospitals and doctor's offices traveling in those early open air primitive roadsters all across the USA on less than ideal roads. This position probably came available through connections which his father had.

As he traveled into every state around the country he collected automobile license plates from each, displaying the collection on the rear wall of his garage. As a child, I remember standing and viewing his collection, thinking Grandpa has been to a lot of places and traveled a lot of miles. He had traveled a very unusual number of miles for that period of time.

Silent Tears

In 1918, Grandma Nanny and the two children traveled by train to Helena, Montana to meet Grandpa Garfield, hoping to spend some badly needed family time. Their time together would be very short. Mother would make reference to the fact that Papa, as she called him, was always gone and never home. The family had also moved around a lot with no place to call their own.

After the short Montana visit, Grandma and the two children went to Sheridan, Wyoming, renting a house and living there for a year. At the end of that year they returned to North Carolina, staying with family for another two years while Grandpa continued to represent the pharmaceutical company doing the required traveling.

I have no clues about the whys of this next move of Grandma and the children. They boarded the train in Sparta, North Carolina sometime in 1921 and headed north to Didsbury, Alberta. Grandma rented a house where they lived for three years until 1924. I gathered from some comments which mother made, living with other family members had not gone well. The lengthy absence of Papa, with no real home base, had caused family life to become turbulent. Grandma was an unhappy woman, taking her frustrations out on her daughter. This move was probably an escape in Grandma's view, from an unpleasant family situation to another environment totally away from all extended family where loneliness became the family companion. Apparently, Grandma had enough fond memories of Alberta that she wanted to return.

After leaving the original homestead and returning to Alberta were turbulent years for the family. The long separation of husband and father fostered a real insecurity in my mother which affected her for the rest of her life. Grandma and Grandpa's marriage suffered greatly also. They had drifted apart, staying married for the sake of the children. Grandma had become a very unhappy woman according to mother. With Papa always away from the family, companionship between the spouses really suffered.

Through information which my mother shared with me, I tried to put together a time line of those early family years.

1906---in the spring the family left North Carolina, traveled by train to Alberta to obtain a homestead with their baby daughter, Virginia Edna, who was nine months old at the time.

1909---returned to North Carolina for the birth of their son, William Franklin.

1914---the outbreak of World War I

1915---Grandpa Garfield returned to the United States, obtained a job with a pharmaceutical company based in St. Louis, Missouri, then traveled throughout the US selling medical supplies. Grandma Nanny and the two children moved to Olds, Alberta, renting a house and staying there until there was further word from Grandpa G. The stay lasted for one year.

1916---Grandma Nanny and the children returned to North Carolina staying with relatives. Grandma N also comes down with typhoid fever threatening her life, everyone believing that she would not survive. This stay lasted for about two years.

1918---Grandma Nanny and the children traveled by train to Helena, Montana meeting up with their traveling father and husband. Their goal was to spend some badly needed family time together. After that reconnection Grandma and the children went to Sheridan, Wyoming, living there for a year. Why to Sheridan is an unanswered question.

1919---returned to North Carolina and lived with Grandpa G's family for over a year

1920---Grandma Nanny took the children and returned to Alberta to a small town twelve miles south of Olds where they had lived before. Why she chose this town called Didsbury, staying there for four years, was never explained. I only know that mother talked about her education and graduating from high school in that town. She was very determined to make it into medical school so would study until the town turned off the electricity at 1: AM. She would leave the light switch in the on position so that when the lights came back on at five AM she would be awakened, and then would be able to return to her studies.

1924---Grandma Nanny's father passed away in North Carolina. She inherited enough money to buy a quarter section of land in Eagle Valley, Alberta sometimes referred to as Mound. This property was twenty four miles west and north of Didsbury on the east side of Big Red. (No more having to ford the river!) This brought some badly needed stability to their family. In time the family was able to acquire another quarter section of land adjacent to this original property.

Grandpa Garfield did not join the family at this acquired farm. He knew farm work would be more than he could physically endure. During that same year he obtained a job with the Alberta government as a game warden. His traveling throughout the US would come to an end but would be traveling around the province. Family life with him included was not being restored. Mother's comment about their family life was that, "Papa was always gone." She always referred to her father as "Papa".

It was during this time of working for the Alberta government that he started the Alberta Fish Hatchery in Crandon. This was a hatchery specifically for the breeding and raising of trout.

1946---Grandpa retired from his position with the Alberta Government after having worked for them for twenty two years.

1947---Grandpa and Grandma along with their son William and his wife Margaret returned to North Carolina for a family reunion. This was their final trip to North Carolina.

As I review the information received from my mother, I marvel at their lifestyle for their time in history. The mobility which they experienced as a family, reads more like life in the twenty first century, except they were minus the twenty first century means of mobility and conveniences. They experienced mobility during the automobile's beginnings and less than luxury rail travel. The auto was in its infancy, yet Grandpa traveled all over the USA in these bumpy roadsters that were anything but comfortable or speedy. They were almost a nuclear family before the word nuclear was ever heard of.

During those years which my grandparents spent apart, by my account, amounted to approximately thirty years. Lack of family togetherness along with no support of extended family, drained the life blood of the family unit's cohesiveness. Mother, in making reference to those days of separation, spoke of fears and anxiety on the part of Grandma. These insecurities which the family felt left some long lasting effects, especially on my mother. Her personal insecurities were deeply rooted and lasted her lifetime. Currently, it is a well known fact that instability in the family life breeds insecurities in the children.

Grandpa sent money home to support them, so indeed their expenses were taken care of. He was faithful in that respect according to my mother. Grandma and the children had their financial needs met. He would take breaks from traveling, when it was possible, to spend time with the family. However, those stays were always short and never enough according to mother.

The children were starved for Papa attention. I'm sure he was family time starved himself. I don't know what options existed for him during the generation in which they lived. In light of the very difficult circumstances, I have to give him credit for persevering.

Grandma spent her time on the land which she purchased with her inheritance money. Moving from that rented house in Didsbury to the land she was able to purchase, brought her some stability for the first time in her married life. She lived there with her two children, growing a garden, raising turkeys and chickens. Her son, William, whom we called Uncle Bill, got his start in farming working the land which his mother had been able to purchase. In time he established himself on an adjacent property raising his herd of beef cattle, chickens for meat and eggs, as well as thoroughbred race horses. My mother married a local rancher's son, so her life continued in a similar direction.

The move from town to an immersed country lifestyle brought much needed stability to the whole family. This opened the door for their father and husband to discontinue his traveling around the USA. His working for the Alberta Government as a game warden in the Land, Forest, and Wildlife Division brought some needed changes to his life, as well. At least the whole family was now all located within the same province and family visits could be more frequent, longer, and a little more convenient, with this change. In reality, that increased family time together did not improve that much until the day of his retirement.

This new career was like a homecoming for Grandpa Garfield. He would be working in the outdoor environment that he felt so at home in. He would be working within the realm of his interest with the possibility of making a contribution to the sport of fishing in the Province of Alberta.

Garfield Samuel Thompson

The Man I Knew

"**Welllll** --- WHO DO WE HAVE HERE?" That greeting followed with a great big barrel hug, was Grandpa's way of saying to us grandkids that he was thrilled to see us. We were just as thrilled to be in his presence. His warmth of spirit, smile, and gregarious persona reflected his southern US style of hospitality. This was a characteristic he carried with him throughout his lifetime.

I loved that characteristic of his personality. His welcoming spirit made everyone feel at home immediately with the conversation picking up where it ended during the last visit. He made his company the object of his attention and they felt it. The warmth of his presence would permeate a room like a lighted lamp dispelling the shadows in every corner. His conversation was always a shared experience, with the gift of being a good listener, sprinkled with his cosmopolitan southern country style of humor.

One of my favorite memories of him was during an afternoon visit to their home with my mother. Grandpa was very kid-like himself and loved to tease. He was sitting in his rocker and I was sitting on his lap, which I often would do. He noticed a cut on my finger which I had incurred earlier. He pulled out his pocket knife, of which he was never without, and said to me "Let me cut that out." Of course I hollered "NO" but I knew he was joking and I loved his attention. This was such a simple act, but was important to me that I have long held those moments as fond memories. I still see us in his favorite rocker with me on his lap and the laughter we shared. I wish I could thank him for his gift of himself that he shared that day. In light of future experiences, it was a priceless gift, simple, but priceless. Later, another experience with a different grandparent spoke volumes reflecting a completely different value system.

Speaking of that rocker, it is with me as of this day. Grandpa would sit in it and whittle away creating his wooden eggs for his egg laying hens' nests. He did so much whittling that he wore a hole with his pocket knife on the leading edge of the rocker's seat. When I inherited it from my mother I had it restored. The hole was filled in with some wood putty. In fact, that rocker sits next to me as I write. In my grandparent's house that rocker would sit near the kitchen table and I can still see it there in my mind. This rocker is also where some of my earliest memories of Grandpa begin. To this day, sitting in that rocker helps my creative juices start to flow. Maybe it's my personal steroid.

Another fond memory I have of him and one that I wish I could thank him for is the time he spent with my own daughter, his great-granddaughter, when she was just one year old. I had traveled by rail with her arriving in Alberta at the end of June. Grandpa was about eighty two at the time. He spent a lot of time following her around pretending to ride along on a broom with her. Having a partner on this imaginary ride brought a big sparkle to her eyes, enjoying every minute of his attention. In his playful spirit he also spent time wheeling her around in the old wheelbarrow. She loved that too. Grandpa was like the pied piper as children loved being in his presence.

Grandpa also had his batch of foxhounds, that's what he called them anyway. He would bring them to my parent's farm for the purpose of keeping the coyotes away from their herd of sheep, a big problem that my parents had. These were as large as brush wolves and when slaughtering these defenseless animals the result would be a very ugly sight. Foxhounds were great trackers. When they picked up a coyote's scent they would be gone for hours. We could hear them barking all up and down Big Red as well as in the forest land west of the sheep fields. Using these dogs helped to clear out the coyote population for a time. The sheep would be safer again for a while. The coyotes seemed to move to a different territory where it was more peaceful. However, they always returned.

    He had a unique way of calling his dogs off their hunt. Blowing through a large hollowed out steer horn to make this low wooooo sound would be a sound his hounds would recognize as a command to come home. It was unique to me, but actually an ancient method from time long gone.

Grandpa was fifty nine years old when I was born. The absence of his presence was there in my very early years. For my mother, he was away for all of her youth except for those short visits during his travels. Her Papa was never around. I was nine years old when he permanently retired from the Alberta government. Retirement enabled him to be permanently home with his family. My mother was ten years old when he started to travel for the pharmaceutical company. I was the fortunate one to have as much time with him as I did. My mother and her brother were Papa-time deprived. I was able to know and experience him for twenty plus years before he left this earth. Mother and her brother experienced his absence for approximately thirty years. They had dearly missed him during their growing up years. It was not until she was forty years old that the family was able to reconnect with a consistent frequency. She also spoke of the effect these long absences had on her parent's marriage and the family as a whole. My response, "I can only imagine".

    I was the privileged one. I had the opportunity to know him after having gone through the firestorms of life which brings maturity to a personhood. I was able to witness his gracious demeanor to everyone he would meet. Articulate, intelligent, culturally adaptable, gregarious, ready to converse with anyone with ease, and possessing a listening ear with the ability to make anyone feel comfortable in his presence. A story-teller with a quiet low-key sense of humor which reflected his southern roots. A true example of always being a gentleman but also exuding a personal standard that had its influence.

The following is a memory of my grandfather which has influenced me to this day. We never know how one little incident can leave a life- long impression on someone else. I doubt he ever knew his personal standard left such a legacy to be remembered by.

My brother was about sixteen and I would have been about eleven. The two of us were visiting my grandparents. I don't remember the details of our activity, however, I starkly remember that we were standing in front of his garage. Apparently my brother used some slang language; the exact words I did not hear. I do know that it was only slang language and not foul words that he used. However, I did hear with no uncertainty, the verbal chastisement that my brother received from my grandfather regarding this matter.

His chastisement went something like this. "When you use slang language you are revealing to others your ignorance, your inability to express yourself intelligently, and use the English language correctly." Those words hung in my brain leaving me with a "WOW" feeling. That sounded so negative to my mind. When I relate that story to others no one believes me. He probably swears when you are not around they say. Somewhere along the line I would have heard a verbal slip-up. When slang is part of your vocabulary it will come out when your guard is down. He has forever been my standard for verbal communication and I thank him for that. In this day where foul language is so prevalent and thought of as being cool I think of my grandfather and wish to myself that there were a lot more people like him.

Having been a witness to the life of a man whom I can call Grandpa, during those short twenty something years gave me a glimpse into the life of a person I feel very fortunate to have known. When I try to combine the stories that my mother shared with me, along with the personal experiences I have been blessed to be a part of, her stories have become much more than just stories that I heard as a child. I didn't have any reason to doubt them, it's just that all they were stories and not yet personal. I had not matured enough within myself to value that part of my own history and identity.

As I have thought about and recalled Mother's stories, my family history has become much more real. While I have tried to put down on paper my memories of them, their history has become part of the personalities which I knew. A wholeness has taken place to provide me with a completeness of the personalities which I valued so much as a young girl growing up. Their lives as young people, I can compare to my own youthful days. Their struggles as parents and their daily living, I can compare to my own days in the same stage of life. Their golden years, I can understand more clearly now. Grasping a picture of the totality of their lives is giving me a completeness that I never realized was missing. The richness of their stories, and their legacies too full to be allowed to be lost by history flipping the unending pages of time.

Why Grandpa chose to spend so much time away from his family to provide for them comes to us in the knowledge of their time, place, and circumstances. War, health problems, and jobs are universal challenges and always provides individual circumstances to be dealt with. How these challenges are dealt with is a measure of who we are. I am grateful for my grandfather's perseverance and I'm also glad that I didn't have to walk in his shoes, because his life was no picnic. However, I do believe he enjoyed his life to the best of his ability. To me that is success. I never sensed any bitterness on his part but an appreciation for that which he believed to be important, at least most of the time. Spiritually his connectedness to God came through listening to the Billy Graham Radio Hour. During his last year of life that became ultra important to him.

Silent Tears

Grandpa's contribution to the Fish, Game and Wildlife Department in the Alberta Government has not been expounded upon. I will include an article that was published by Land, Forest, and Wildlife Magazine sometime in the early 1960's. Unfortunately the date of the article is missing from the clipping that was mailed to me when living in Milwaukee. This article gives a fair description of Grandpa's contribution to the sport of wildlife recreation. The following article is taken word for word from the publication mentioned. However, some of the information written in the first paragraph is not quite correct but not enough to invalidate the remaining publication.

Father of Lock Leven Trout

Courtesy of "Land, Forest, Wildlife Magazine"

Garfield S. Thompson brought his wife to the Mound district northeast of Sundre, Alberta, in 1906. Here they established the farm-stead that is their home today. Here they have lived and raised their family with the exception of eight years spent at the Raven rearing station while Mr. Thompson was employed by the provincial government. One son, William, lives nearby and still helps his father with the chores at the home farm. A daughter, Mrs. Edna Fletcher, is the wife of a neighboring farmer. There are two grandchildren.

In 1925 the fishermen in the vicinity of Red Deer, Olds, Innisfail, and Didsbury, looking at the many quiet streams in the country west of them, wondered why their fishing was limited to pike, bull trout and whitefish. Just as sportsmen do today, these anglers asked their government if something could be done to increase their selection of trout stream product. Their government was sympathetic but not quite sure how to begin such a project. Garfield Thompson who had participated in many of their discussions recalled seeing a trout in Montana called the brown or Lock Leven trout. The environment, in which it seemed to thrive there, appeared to be very much like the streams of Garfield's own country. He asked himself and the government officials of the day if brown trout stocking in streams of the Red Deer and Clearwater River systems would not be worth a trial. The government agreed, and in 1926 hired Garfield Thompson to work as a fisheries warden in the district in which he lived with the understanding that he would attempt to introduce these trout to

Silent Tears

the streams. Brown trout eggs were obtained in 1927 and incubated at the trout hatchery in Banff. The first fingerlings that reached Garfield in 1927 were planted in three streams; these were Grant, Castle and Schrader creeks, all tributaries of the Red Deer River. These plantings were the initial step in the provision of one of the most stable trout fisheries in Alberta.

During the years following 1927 Garfield Thompson, with the help of Jack Martin at the Banff hatchery conducted a strenuous and effective trout planting program within an area covering almost 3000 square miles. What is more, his work was done at a time when roads were primitive or non- existent and when horse and wagon was used more often than truck. Many of the waters into which Garfield dipped his pail Alberta anglers are still pulling fat lock leven from many of these places.

Garfield Thompson retired from government service at sixty five years of age in 1947, yet today he is youthful looking and spry. When he talks about his early fisheries endeavors his shoulders become often straighter and his eyes gleam. He recalls with a nostalgic sigh the seven mile pack horse trip he took in 1928 to plant Eagle Lake. Another time on a trip to Moose Creek, his vehicle broke down near Swan Creek, so he planted his load in the latter stream and personally took brown trout from Swan Creek a few years later. All stones creek is approximately 125 miles from the Raven station. Garfield was sent there with a load of brown trout in the early 1930's but bogged down in the vicinity of Shunda Creek, right at Nordegg. Again he had no alternative but to release his trout and, to date, Shunda Creek remains one of the most productive brown trout streams in Alberta. This in spite of many years of intensive angling carried out by residents of the thriving Nordegg mining community.

An early planting in the Nordegg district served to illustrate to some novice trout fishing residents how difficult the brown trout is to catch. A pail full of trout had been deposited in a small catch basin near the town. In the following year the Nordegg anglers mournfully told Garfield that only one brown trout had survived the planting. How did they know? Because constant angling failed to produce any fish, yet when they walked along the shore they always saw one trout. In fact, it appeared as though the trout followed them for no matter which part of the lake *they approached this trout was always there. They assumed on the basis of a law of averages that there could not possibly be any more trout in the water because none were being caught by the dozens of the fishermen who were attempting to do so. Garfield realized at once that there were many trout alive in the lake and that the anglers were seeing different trout all the time. He showed them how to catch brown trout and, before long, Nordegg anglers were reaping a gratifying harvest from their little pond.*

Garfield Thompson's research methods were simple. To evaluate a stream for planting purposes, he merely looked for bull trout. If many were present in the stream he did not plant it, if they appeared to be absent he did. Naturally he became a very proficient trout fisherman himself. Practically all the tricks used by successful anglers to catch Alberta brown trout are known to him. Just how many frustrated anglers he has taught these techniques to is unknown, undoubtedly a great number. Perhaps throughout the years, he has best of all displayed not only initiative and endeavor but patience, goodwill and a philosophical acceptance of nature, all essential graces of the true trout fisherman and dedicated naturalist. Present and future Alberta fishermen will never be able to repay Garfield Thompson for his contribution to their sport.

This report from the, "Land, Forest, Wildlife Magazine," truly reflects the love of a naturalist's lifestyle that my grandfather had fallen in love with which became his life blood, his tonic, and his total focus. His early experiences surviving those Montana winters dealing with his health was a total emersion experience helping him become dauntless in the face of nature.

He was the one who founded the Raven Brooding Hatchery in Caroline, Alberta, after discovering the artesian springs while traveling around this 3000 square mile assignment as a warden. After getting the government's okay to develop ponds from these springs, this hatchery became very productive and is still actively producing hatchlings today. This was an immense benefit for sport fishing in the province of Alberta.

Silent Tears

    This love of nature and particularly his love for fishing became an out of balance focus of his life which I will explain with my next Grandpa story.

    My grandparents were living in a large farmhouse with no amenities such as running water, indoor plumbing, or a central heating system. Their only source of heat was a wood burning cook stove and a tall cast iron belly heater. This wasn't unusual since none of the neighbors were any better off.

    Grandma had purchased this land and house with inherited money from her father's estate. She had some changes made that better suited her idea of a workable floor plan. The old living room became a bedroom and the old kitchen became the living room etc. etc. A second story was added with three bedrooms and an attic. She even added a portico to the front of the house providing a touch of North Carolina influence. I never did see anyone sitting out there relaxing or enjoying the beautiful vista available because of their hillside building sight.

    With added space the old farmhouse had now become quite large. The new bedroom had wood planking floors minus any kind of finish. The new living room became the most completed with varnished hardwood flooring, tastefully painted drywall, and the finishing touch of crown molding, giving the living room a classy feel not replicated in other country homes in the area. The davenport was upholstered in a dark brown coarse fiber upholstery fabric that would resemble bear hair more than any upholstery fabric I have ever seen. She probably found it at an auction as they were her go-to places for everything she owned.

Hanging trophy-sized wildlife heads dominated the living room. The moose's large glass eyes and huge rack of horns would not let your eyes wander to much else that occupied other spaces. These were Grandpa's proud rifle shots, preserved as a memorial to those mountain expeditions with his hunting buddies. (These massive heads ended up hanging on the walls of the local museum along with their stories) Grandma either was a good sport or just tolerated those stuffed heads for a lack of other wall décor options.

Settling into retirement life with their lives finally reunited on a permanent basis, Grandma wanted Grandpa to help lay some linoleum over the wood planking floor in their bedroom. She had purchased this floor covering several years prior in the hope that someday it would get laid. With the floor laying project well under way, the phone rang. Grandpa got to the phone first. His friend was calling to see if he wanted to go fishing. Grandpa immediately packed his fishing gear and walked out the door leaving the project unfinished. Grandma's linoleum laying project came to an end never reaching a state of completion with the remainder of the linoleum roll standing in the corner of their bedroom, forever.

In view of their lives as a whole, the time in which they lived, the relationship which they had, the circumstances which they adapted to, the values which influenced their lives can be left with the thought, "ENOUGH SAID".

Nanny Edna Thompson-- Nee--Abshire

The Woman I Knew

"OH SHUCKS," was one of her sayings if things weren't going right at the moment along with a list of others for good measure. "I've got an itchy nose so company is coming." She might throw in, "You're going to kiss a fool," or "A bird in hand is worth two in the bush", "A penny saved is a penny earned," "A stitch in time saves nine," "Haste makes waste," and "You never miss the water until the well runs dry." "If you dream of a marriage there is going to be a funeral," "If you dream of a death, there is going to be a marriage." "Black cat crossing your path," or a "Dog howling at midnight," gave ominous predictions.

Superstitions were a part of her mind set. If she had any of those dreams which unsettled her mind, you were sure to hear about it. Her emotional turmoil could last for numerous days until her nerves had time to settle convincing her that nothing dreadful would happen to either family or friends.

When there was a thunderstorm approaching, you had to be sure you were wearing rubber boots in case lightning struck the house. This kind of protection was certain to keep everyone safe. You must wear a coat or sweater outside and keep your feet dry to avoid catching a cold. These would be admonishments you could expect to receive. To be respected by those whom you did not know very well, you were to "Put your nose in the air." Whatever that meant and not carrying much meaning with it,

I never did figure that one out. Snobbery or arrogance was not apparent in her life.

These sayings and superstitions which she had absorbed over a period of time, seemed to be her guide- posts for dealing with daily living. I never did know her to be a spiritual person who went to church or sought spiritual insights. During their twilight years my grandparents listened to the Billy Graham Hour on their old battery operated radio. Any spiritual insights which might have been absorbed probably would have come through his ministry.

Grandma was fifty-five years old when I was born. Any memory that takes place in a child's mind can be foggy but as time evolves the memory becomes clearer and more vivid. That is the way it was for me with the memories of my grandmother.

I was about seven years old when I became aware of her beautiful auburn hip-length hair which had never been cut. She wore it in a large braided bun held in place with those old fashioned hair pins. This style was the only one she had ever known nor was she mindful of ever making a change. When I would visit I was allowed to undo this braid, untangle those silky auburn strands, and let my fingers glide through all the thickness with her large toothed comb. I was so awed by the color, thickness, and length; in my young mind her hair resembled the fullness of a horse's mane.

Along with this beautiful crown that Grandma was blessed with were a lot of freckles that covered her from head to toe. Never commenting for or against them, I guess she was resigned to being freckled. Her copper brown eyes, high cheek bones, mass of freckles, and auburn hair made for a very enviable appearance. To me as a child, her coloring was beautiful and made me happy I inherited her eyes and some of her freckles along with her high cheek bones. Her copper brown eyes were passed along to my two sons as well.

Grandma also loved to cook. Even though her kitchen remained primitive, she still managed to turn out memorable cuisine which I easily recall.

Her wood burning stove ate a lot of wood before it was ever hot enough to bake anything. Getting the fire going after carrying wood in from the outdoors, stuffing the fire box, and blowing on the flames to create a flickering light took a lot of time and energy before the cooking even got started.

Heat generated by these wood hungry fire boxes also provided ambient heat for the rest of the kitchen and other shared spaces. Warmth could be felt close to the heat source but always much cooler the further you moved away and again much cooler around the room's perimeter. These varying temperatures caused one to dream and wish for central heating.

Grandma's kitchen conveniences remained on the primitive side. One small double door built in cabinet for immediate use items provided minimal storage. The kitchen table was her work space for any food preparation. She often mentioned the desire for a big kitchen with lots of counter space. With her love for cooking and gift of hospitality those facilities were a dream to be dreamed but knowing in her mind that would never come about.

Her real storage was what she called her storeroom, the size of a small bedroom located just off the kitchen. It was a less than desirable room with unpainted walls, bare wood plank floors, and limited lighting. No convenient light switch on the wall existed for ambient lighting. The room was very dark with one small north window. Entering the room you either waited for your eyes to adjust to the inadequate light or you carried one of those old fashioned kerosene lamps in one hand, hoping you could use the free one to bring out whatever you went in to get. Those old lamps gave off less light than a dim flashlight. This room had absolutely no eye appeal but was where she stored her cooking equipment and supplies.

Her flour and sugar came in large fifty pound cloth sacks. Definitely a size you could not throw over your shoulder. That size of bag was readily available for those who purchased in bulk. These bulky sacks sat on the floor in front of the shelves becoming an obstacle for reaching higher stored items. Obviously they were too large to fit anywhere else but on the floor. Moving these massive bags required some muscle that came from other country heavy weight jobs, like carrying wood. I guess with all the physical labor they did on a daily basis moving those heavy bags was not a problem.

Those fabric sacks were later used to make everyday items. Some of the fabric had beautiful print designs which Grandma used for making her housedresses, aprons, dish towels, and quilt tops. Nothing was ever wasted. Everything was used or reused in some way. Frugality was the watch word that touched every aspect of her life.

Root vegetables and canned produce from the garden were all stored in the dirt cellar under the house. A path through Grandma's store room led you to the entrance of that storage area camouflaged by a large hinge-less propped door. This under the house space kept the produce from freezing during those cold Canadian winters. Removing that propped door and climbing down a ladder was the only way to enter this cellar, however, I was never very inclined to investigate to see it for myself. I envisioned the place to be a good cover for mice, spiders, and possibly bats. Needless to say, that was one area in their home that I never visited nor desired to. I wasn't curious about it either as envisioning those critters kept me from going past that propped cellar door.

Even though Grandma's kitchen facilities were very inconvenient, she managed to provide a welcoming spirit to all who visited. She found a way to prepare a good meal, bake a tasty cake, and serve tea in her bone china cups doing it all with graciousness. (Those bone china cups were gifts received from out of town visiting friends) A couple of her specialties she became known for were English plum pudding that graced her table at Christmas time and her tomato bread. Everyone raved about her tomato bread but no one thought to get her recipe before she passed, thus the method of making that bread became a mystery. No one was able to reproduce it with the same texture and flavor which she was able to do.

A very special memory I have of Grandma and Grandpa's hospitality as they worked together to make this meal special was their breakfast. This was their specialty for any overnight or early morning visitor. It was simple but very memorable. It was their combined effort in making you feel your presence was important to them, a reflection of the kind of hospitality they desired to project. It was who they were, always gracious.

Rising at six in the morning, whether summer or winter, it was always the same. Tackling the fire project in both the wood burning cook stove and the pot belly space heater came first. With both fires roaring and stove pipes popping as you heard them heating up, Grandma would go to her store room. There she would get her flour to make her famous, to me, baking powder biscuits. Grandpa would be peeling apples for hot applesauce, then shortly he would busy himself frying his bacon. Freshly baked biscuits with hot applesauce along with fried bacon were a breakfast sent from heaven being made especially for my brother and me. This country style breakfast made with their hands brings back some very warm memories.

The most precious life lesson I received from them was the gift of themselves given in a simple way. They were money poor but rich in their spirits which they shared with their grandkids and others. How fortunate I have been to be the beneficiary of their spirits. They had their own life's journey that had accomplished its own molding of their character. They now had insights to what was really important in life. Unfortunately, I never conveyed to them during their lifetime my appreciation of their legacy but took it for granted. Unfortunately, we don't recognize the value of the moment until it's removed from our lives.

Visiting with my grandmother in my early teens, gave me a chance to hear from her own lips some of her own girlhood dreams. She shared with me how she had loved wearing hats and how she had wanted to become a milliner. Circumstances had directed her life in a different direction and her dream never materialized. Every picture which Grandma was in she could easily be identified by the size of her hat. She managed to look smashing in those very large hats that stylish women wore in her day. She would no doubt have been a great milliner with her great sense of fashion, even though she was living a non- fashionable lifestyle. Living in the hills of western Alberta, where most women adorned themselves in homestead country attire, was not conducive to her sense of fashion. She managed to maintain that sense even as she aged. She amazed me how she was able to remain so cosmopolitan. Unfortunately, life can cause us to lose our dreams if we aren't careful. In Grandma's day, options for women were limited. However, she did have a different dream of remaining stylish wherever she went. She stood alone in that. Style and class were important to her.

Since she was unable to pursue her millinery dreams she focused on developing other creative skills. These went unnoticed until she started to show me some of her creations. She had built storage cabinets for herself and others. Using her hammer and saw storage became a reality for different rooms in the house. This old farm house was devoid of storage so she decided to solve that problem. She didn't leave these cabinets as raw wood as each received a coat of enamel and her personal selection of hardware. As she was showing me some of her creations the declaration was made that if she was a man her projects would have been houses and barns. That thought was very believable.

Grandma didn't limit herself to making cabinets. My parents had a sheep ranch. At shearing time wool was very abundant. Grandma received from my mother several freshly shorn fleeces of wool. Grandma would hand-wash the wool, carefully laying it out on a big sheet to air dry. After the drying process was completed, she would take her cards (a type of comb especially for raw wool), and again carefully laying the now carded wool on those previously washed and sewn together flour and sugar sacks.

She would sandwich the wool between the cotton sacks then bind them all together with a course cotton thread. These were not tied but quilted together, Grandma-style.

Family members were the beneficiary of her many hours, months, and years of quilting labor. I personally received about nine of her quilts which I have shared with my own family using duvet covers to finish them off. These wool quilts cannot be outdone for warmth and comfort in winter months. Today wool quilts aren't even available unless you go to an exclusive website with the price being over four hundred dollars and I am not able to compare the quality.

Memorable times where we could share heart to heart with each other in girl talk style are in the category of "we don't appreciate it until we lose it." When Grandma was seventy four she had a very serious stroke and life for her was never the same. Her beautiful auburn hair, now mixed with gray, had to be cut for the convenience of care. She was faced with a style that was so unfamiliar to her. Perms became a solution helping her to maintain a manageable hair style. Another side effect of the stroke was a change in her memory. Her memory recovered greatly but never to the same level. Medicine in her era didn't have the know-how to avoid that serious illness.

Paging through her old recipe book, I saw that all the pages are hand-written in her own penmanship. Her recipes are a collection from friends and acquaintances, recording the name of the person the recipe was received from, and the date of the occasion when used. Most were similar to recipes we would use currently, but she used much more butter, cream, eggs, and sugar; ingredients we try to use less of today. There were a couple of recipes which I have chosen to record that reflected the creative mind which Grandma possessed. I am rewriting the recipes in Grandma's style.

Strawberry Sandwiches
Mash strawberries add sugar place in an aluminum or granite colander so the juice will drain out. Butter two slices of bread, put strawberries between and cut in strips about 1 ¾ inches wide and about 4 inches long. Arrange neatly on a fancy plate and decorate with a bunch of strawberry leaves and strawberry flowers here and there. The fruit should remain in colander for a few hours till juice is drained out.

Goose-berry Fool
Put 2 quarts of gooseberries in a sauce pan with one quart of water. When they turn yellow drain water off and mash into a pulp through an aluminum colander or mash with a fork. Sweeten and set to cool put yolks of four eggs, beaten into 2 quarts of milk. Stir it until it begins to simmer, add a little nutmeg. Stir into the cool gooseberries half this quantity makes a good dish full do not boil milk and eggs as they will curdle.

I found a tip for whipped cream---Add a teaspoon of gelatine to one pint of whipped cream and it will stand up indefinitely.

Continuing my paging through her recipe collection, I found the following:

Vinegar Pie
1 cup sugar
1 tablespoon of each flour and butter
3 tablespoons of vinegar
1 cup of cold water
Yolks of four eggs beat all together and boil till thick
Will make filling for 2 pies frost with the whites.

Silent Tears

Christmas Pudding---served first time in 1949 (This was a yearly tradition at Christmas after that)
1 cup suet, 2 cups flour, 1 cup soda biscuit crumbs, 1 cup of raisins, ¾ cup citron peel, 1 cup molasses, 1 cup buttermilk, 1 cup currants, 1 teaspoon soda, 1/2 teaspoon salt, 1 teaspoon cinnamon, 1 teaspoon nutmeg, 4 eggs, Rub suet into flour well, add salt, breadcrumbs, fruit and spices, add molasses soda and milk. Then add to mixture eggs, steam three to four hours in a small covered pot set into a larger pot of boiling water. Do not have enough water so it will boil over into the pudding, nuts maybe added to pudding.

Pudding Sauce
1 cup sugar--brown ½ of it mix with tablespoon of flour with other half of sugar add 2 cups of boiling water and the browned sugar boil till all is dissolved then add sugar and flour let come to a boil flavor with cinnamon add tablespoon of butter.
   Next time she made this receipt she added sour cream

A few more gems I found which reflected the era in which they lived.
   Treating a cough---The juice of five lemons with a pint of honey. Take often
   Croup----warm whiskey or brandy weakened with water and sweetened
   Boot Grease---Boil together 2 parts pine tar + 3 parts cod liver oil. Rub in boots while still hot.
   For Rheumatism---Boil Tamarac bark as it comes from the tree not bothering to take rosin off. Drink for water
   Earache---Rub castor oil inside and outside of ear. Warm the oil.
   These were nuggets of interest to relish. Home remedies were the foundation for ailments and daily well being.
   I remember seeing my grandparents use kerosene as a disinfectant around the house when someone visited whom they did not know. A

watchful eye was at work taking note of everything the visitor touched. All would be swabbed with a cloth dipped in kerosene. Chair seats, the back of the chair, door knobs, and any flat surface were not spared. Any dishes used were boiled in a water bath. They were concerned about some disease being spread and then being infected. My grandfather was a very gregarious person but was extremely careful about any body contact with people who he did not know. Never a hug or a hand on the shoulder, maybe a handshake but that was avoided if it was possible.

Turning a few more pages of her recipe book, I noted a couple of recipes that reflect their way of life and decided to include them.

Treatment for colic in horses or cattle
1 cup of molasses
1 or 2 yeast cakes dissolved in warm water
Add molasses to yeast make it into about a quart by adding warm water let it stand until it works
Put in a warm place on stove but don't let it get hot
When it starts to work give to horses

Poultice----from a nurse for sore throat
Spread lard thickly over a thin cloth then sprinkle on dry mustard fold poultice into half of its size and apply to throat Can be applied to chest for cold Poultice maybe kept on till it dries this may be 2 or 3 days if put on chest for bronchitis a fresh poultice may be put on

The following page is a recipe giving us a sample of her own handwriting. Her penmanship reflects the written form of her day.

> **81**
>
> English Plum Pudding (for Mr. Clark
> from Mrs. Chambers)
>
> 1 lb. raisins
> 1 " currants
> 1 " chopped suet rubbed with four Tablespoons fl.
> 1 " white sugar
> 1 " bread crumbs
> ½ lb. blanched almonds
> ½ " mixed peel
> 1 teaspoon salt
> 1 g. grated nutmeg
> 3 teaspoons b. powder
> 1 cup brandy or fruit juice
> 4 well beaten eggs
> a little sweet cream
> steam about ¾ an hour.

Grandma Nanny's Handwriting

Grandpa Garfield and Grandma Nanny's Home site

Their building site was truly unique, a city home dweller's dream of a country abode. A site that was carved out of a woodland covered terraced hillside, with a large valley below where your eyes could stretch like a rubber band to the valley's far edges being bordered by another foothill range. This large hill was a segment of a foothill range which extended for miles. Foothills seem to provide an approach to mountains, wandering in different directions, varying in height and steepness, presenting themselves as irregular forms with much variety.

This hillside had been scarred and leveled off enough to provide a building site plus enough space for a footpath between the house and the hill bank. A vertical bank was cut out of the hillside to form this path. In order to accommodate ease for foot traffic, loosely laid planks formed the base of the walkway covering a dirt foundation. There was a need for these specifics. This path had to be wide enough for easy passage when carrying buckets of water from the well located at the rear of the house. This was a daily chore that required replenishing the home's water supply for all household needs.

Walking out their front door and standing on their walkway, your eyes wanted to absorb the valley's offerings. Trees, brush, and open tilled fields, furnished the scenery. A county road made its slice through the valley establishing the eastern boundary of my grandparent's property. This mixture of topography which extended for miles, painted a picture which your eyes never ceased to enjoy.

Silent Tears

The outbuildings and small barn with corrals were all required to adapt themselves to the varying slopes and uneven ground surfaces. Surrounding all the buildings was the large sloping Hereford cow pasture. Cold and uninviting in the winter, but springtime drew one in to enjoy the fresh green grass, new field flowers, freshly leafed poplars, new born baby calves, romping and playing in the warm sunshine.

A constant resident in that pasture were my uncle's large Hereford bulls. Their size and stares were very intimidating, but never seemed to be aggressive. However, the intimidated feelings you possessed made for an awareness of a needed safety zone in case an emergency occurred.

A very memorable feature of their home was actually the interior. Three large windows were joined together making one very large one. These were part of Grandma Nanny's remodeling plan by having them placed in the wall of the kitchen which faced the pathway's scarred out hillside, giving an unobstructed view of nature and all that it has to offer. The hill was too high and too close to the bay window for any blue sky to be seen but was bountifully clothed with the stuff of nature. Only tree trunks would come into view being surrounded with underbrush and seasonal wild flowers that made for a natural blanket right down to the planking pathway. Nature's view was always present through these extensive glass window panes.

In spring the wild flowers would show their color, summer displayed its green, then fall with its colored splendor of copper tones, and of course, winter presented itself with bountiful kisses of white frosting which made you dream of spring again. Sometimes a wild rabbit would come down low enough on the hillside providing a full view of itself from the kitchen. Occasionally a deer would meander its way through this paradise of nature providing a photo moment for anyone fortunate enough to be present when they appeared. On a few occasions, I even remember seeing colorful partridges, studying the kitchen activity, as they peered through the windows silhouetted by the white background which winter provides in abundance. Unfortunately, no one ever captured these scenes on camera, but now they live on being captured in my memory.

The window size was approximately five feet high and about twelve feet long. Most construction plans would have designed a much smaller area of glass. Grandma had the vision and creativity during her house redo project to take advantage of this picturesque scene so that it could be a part of her daily life.

A well with a hand pump was located at the rear of the house sourcing the water needed for daily use. A tall ladder attached to the wells' inside wall enabled one to climb down for well inspection. Grandma was concerned about a mouse falling in and contaminating the water even though the well head was solidly capped. She had good reason to be concerned after her typhoid illness experience, an illness caused by contaminated water.

Sometimes Grandpa would don his wooden yoke, heading for a gushing spring which flowed out of the side of the hill about a quarter mile away. He would walk this quarter-mile; fill his buckets bringing them back with fresh cold spring drinking water. All I can say is there is no drinking water as good as that cold fresh spring liquid. It was the best ever.

Visiting their home, you approached the house by first driving down a spruce tree-lined half-mile dirt road. Making the final curve of the drive, the first thing you would see was Grandpa's woodpile of logs. Some pieces would be split and ready to make fire while others remained in log form, all lying near his garage. Your eyes would do their normal sweep, checking for differences, or your ears listening for a friendly greeting. Grandma's flowers which lined the walkway would soon grab your attention.

In short notice your eyes would turn to face their unpainted, raw wood, two story house. Even though everything you viewed was rustic, simple and neatly maintained with care, an aura of warmth emitted and filled your being. You knew you would be welcomed with that southern hospitality which never was lost, even though much time had gone by since their NC days. That was part of who they were. Grandpa was always the gentleman and Grandma the gracious hostess.

Grandpa lived for twenty years on that property. Grandma resided forty two years. Twenty two of those years was without her husband but had the comfort of her son and daughter living nearby. That was a great comfort to her in her aging years. I never knew her to be a worrying kind of person. However, I gather from comments which my mother made, that during those gypsy-style years, Grandma was not a happy person, taking her frustrations out on the kids, especially my mother. Being able to purchase this quarter section of land with a two room house, brought stability to her life after experiencing so many years of no permanency. Remodeling this farm house and expanding it into a ten room structure was her vision of newness and an expression of her creativity. This land and house gave both of them a place to be together, bringing some sense of re-acquaintance to their marriage.

Living Life in the River Valley

My mother was taken to the hospital by her father and brother at the time of my birth. My mother returned from the hospital the same way she arrived. My father never made the twenty five mile trip to the hospital to welcome me into this world.

Returning from the hospital with me as her newborn, she would learn that my father had thrown out the little bed that was to be mine. How she dealt with this I do not know. I don't recall her ever again making reference to that day. For her, I believe the memory of these circumstances was too painful for her to reminisce in her mind. Never did she ever fill me in on the circumstances of my older brother's birth.

Sharing this bit of information left me with the numb feeling that I really didn't want to know more. As she spoke those words a real feeling of non importance and a spirit of darkness filled my emotions. She never elaborated with anymore information and I never asked.

I was already old enough to know that our family life was not a healthy one as she made reference to the details of my birth. My reaction to this state of numbness, forever kept me from asking questions. I adjusted by learning to listen to mother's words, then internalizing them. This developed into a long term habit of listening and internalizing which would later evolve into a very unhealthy state of mind. The habit I was setting up for myself was truly emotionally self destructive and unrecognized by anyone, including me.

Remembering the feeling that I felt, as she related this bit of family history, took many years before I was able piece together enough information in creating an understandable picture. In time, I came to understand that mother had a real challenge trying to raise two children in a man's world.

This River Valley was the center of life for us as a family. Our farm lay between two foothill ranges. The Big Red Deer River had helped to form the valley by cutting its own path and going wherever it determined itself to go. The contour lines of the valley reflected the river's free will, developing itself over eons of time. During our occupation it had settled itself bordering the western edge of our farm. It left behind lots of rocks in the open fields which kept being unearthed every time my father used his old Case tractor and plow to work the soil, in preparation for seeding his yearly crop of oats and other grains.

Looking down on the valley from the eastern rim was a beautiful vista. Virgin forest land with their deep emerald greens contrasted with the amber grain and ash green hay fields. A no-name country road led to the entrance gate of our farm as well as other farms that lay along the way. Our farmhouse just showed up as a small dot from this beautiful vista point. We could see our neighbor's home-sites on the opposite side located on these high river banks. These neighbors were a short distance yet far away, since Big Red formed this permanent barrier between us.

My parents had managed to obtain 320 acres of land in this valley. One hundred and sixty were purchased from a neighbor; the other acres were given to my father by his father. That clarification came much later. He was given the use, but no title.

The western half of the property was covered with a virgin pine forest, a sprinkling of quaking aspens, poplar trees, as well as silver leaf rabbit brush that grew well in low wetland. Springs which bubbled up through the ground kept the area in a marsh like environment. These springs also formed small ponds which would then flow into the main river bed. Springs bubbling through the ground all along the river bed gave us kids' built-in icy cold short-dip swimming pools. Melting glaciers in the Rocky

Mountains, melting snows, falling rain, and the ever bubbling springs provided a permanent source of water to feed the ever rapid flowing Big Red.

Open tillable fields, forested acres, rabbit brush, and the many bubbling springs along with Big Red provided a multi-faceted environment. This offered great opportunities for activities as well as a wonderful habitat for various kinds of wildlife. Rabbits, brush wolves, deer, bobcats, squirrels, mink, and the occasional black bear and moose made this land their home. Beavers had a great time building their dams since the habitat was perfect for their amazing building skills. What they can do with some mud and sticks is mind-bending. They also enabled those spring pools to flood areas creating extra wetlands for migrating waterfowl.

Big Red also provided the cold water needed for the trout's habitat and recreational fishing. The flooding waters with spring snow melts tended to reduce the trout population, however, someone was always trying to make a catch. In spite of our closeness to the river my father never went fishing so the habit was never established in our immediate family. However, Grandpa Garfield, the professional fisherman, would take us kids on occasion. That was always a treat and an activity that we could enjoy with our grandfather.

We learned some angling skills, such as how not to get your fishhook caught in nearby tree branches or fallen logs in the water. Landing a hooked trout was another lesson we learned. Wearing dark clothing instead of light clothing made you much less visible. You were to always wade in the water upstream and never downstream because the fish would swim against the flow of the water lessening the chances of you being seen by these skittish fish. Trout are easily tipped off to any kind of movement.

Many times we went home with empty nets but that didn't matter. If we did go home with a catch, there would be more lessons to learn. "How do we clean this slippery thing?" After that came the cooking lesson for our catch of the day. That involved the old cast iron pan with added homemade butter over semi-low heat. Another lesson, "How to eat trout without getting a fish bone stuck in your throat." They have way too many fine little bones to contend with. We learned that you eat trout very carefully. After eating our catch, the satisfied feeling we felt was any day spent with Grandpa fishing was a great day.

This river basin with its tributaries offered sport fishing to other anglers as well. Often times acquaintances or strangers would drive down our road, knock on the door asking for permission, then walk through our property back to the river to spend the day. Of course we always said "Yes," as they were never the ones to cause any problems.

This environmental paradise offered another source of recreation; horseback riding. My brother and I would either saddle up or decide to go bareback for an adventure following the river's edge, riding through the silver leafed willows and usually ending up in the pine forest. There our imaginations would kick into high gear. We would engage in our favorite pretend game that some wild animal was chasing us or imagine we were doing the cowboys and Indian thing, spurring our horses' full speed ahead. We would lay our faces and chests flat on the horse's mane using our arms and hands to push away low hanging tree branches as we sped along. Finally after about a mile of pure adrenaline we would bring our horses to a puffing stop with the two of us being totally exhilarated.

While out in the woods on our riding days we would try some tree climbing. One of my favorite activities was to survey the trees looking for just the right tree to climb turning it into a teeter totter activity. The tree had to have a large enough trunk that wouldn't break when climbed or not so rigid that it would not flex. After finding the right tree and climbing as close to the top as possible and waiting for it to bend from my body weight. The right tree would bend low enough allowing my feet to touch the ground, and then I could use my feet and legs in a springing motion to send myself back up to an almost erect position. Over and over this motion would go on until enough was enough.

Selma J. Stroebel

When needing help to mount my big fifteen-hand palomino horse and my older brother wasn't available, I had my own solution. Waiting for my horse to put his head down to eat, I would sit on his head. Of course with a kid on his head my horse would raise it up. Now all I had to do was crawl down his long neck turn around and I'd be ready to go. All I can say is that this trick worked and worked well, it never failed. My horse seemed to adjust to my antics. Ponies were never available for me to ride, so I was required to adapt my mounting techniques.

We stopped riding together when my brother was in his early teens. He began to spend more time with our grandparents and my aunt and uncle. Other concerns were becoming evident interrupting our recreation time together. He was not coping well to my father's problems and not understanding our mother. Seeking other experiences through a lot of time spent with our grandparents seemed to provide a temporary solution for him. Those free time recreational hours have remained in my mind as real positive experiences and memories, helping to soothe those other hours that were filled with a real depth of utter frustration and stress.

This river valley provided a huge theater for God's concert hall. Night time was the time of the day when the nocturnal wildlife made their presence known and the concert would begin.

Just after dusk the brush wolves did a lot of communicating. Their howling pierced the stillness of the night sending an eerie message to one's ears. One pack of brush wolves would communicate with another pack, sometimes on opposite hillsides. Each pack seemed to understand the messages they were sending to the other pack, but to our ears the message was very menacing, visualizing one of our lambs becoming their dinner.

Before long the owls would break any silence with their hooting. I call them the night-time drummers, bringing a rhythm to God's concert hall. We always knew what they would be after, which was any stubborn chicken that insisted on perching in some old pine or poplar tree rather than roosting in the chicken coop where they belonged.

Silent Tears

Big Red could be heard creating its own music. As I lay in my upstairs bedroom with the window wide open, I could hear Big Red's steady hum like stringed instruments playing their waltzes. The swift flow of water over large rocks and boulders in the river bottom created a music that helped to negate some of the other ominous night sounds. Listening to the music provided by Big Red caressed the tired spirit which was ready to end a very full day.

Combining all the night sounds together made for nature's musical symphony which was purely original with no man as a participant. The pureness of it all is irreplaceable, nor can it be duplicated. While as a child on the farm, I took all of this for granted with very little appreciation. I guess that is one way we waste our youth.

The eastern half of our farm was an open field of rich tillable land. The color of the soil was nearly as black as coal. Rich from many years of mineral deposits and vegetation decay provided a great formula for growing different grains and legumes. This soil had not been depleted from years of poor agricultural practices, as Canada was still this new frontier but evolving into another generation of farmers. My parents were part of this new generation of agricultural land keepers.

It was on this land that my father grew his great stands of oats, barley, wheat, or legumes such as alfalfa or sweet clover. From these he gained a sense of pride and success in his own simple way. His planting and harvesting routine was a way of life which he was able to manage fairly well. Driving his antique lug wheeled Case tractor, tilling the black soil, and seeding the different grains gave him a sense of accomplishment. Producing bumper crops, and receiving many compliments on his crop yields was a miracle for him, but we didn't know it at the time.

Mother would complain loud and clear concerning illogical decisions my father would make. Why would he want to drive the sheep to water when they could go on their own? During hot summer days water needs to be available continuously, not a couple times a day. All that takes is installing a fence line that leads to water instead of the fence creating a barrier. Why would he plant the alfalfa legume where the animals can get to it? Alfalfa is deadly to ruminants in its fresh green form.

During discussions regarding these subjects, his reactions were mute. When proceeding to go forward with the project, his decisions were based on personal likes rather than what was expedient. When building the fences he placed them in the direction he wanted them to go just because he liked the direction of the line, not that it was going to cause a lot of inconvenience.

Most of the time he would grow his fields of grain. In some seasons he would decide to grow legumes as well. Fresh green clover and alfalfa, especially alfalfa, are deadly to ruminating livestock. The planted fields were easily in reach of animals if they found an opening in the fence line. If there is a hole there is an uncanny ability to find such, as they love the taste of that rich green stuff. If not that, a gate left open is an invitation to the forbidden. My father was famous for forgetting to close gates.

Emergencies were a daily unwanted visitor, due to this illogical decision making process. No matter how much mother would try to explain the difference between some of his ideas, convenience versus inconvenience, profits versus losses, expedience never seemed to win. Discussions consisted of her talking and his listening to her explanations with little input on his part giving the impression that he did not care that much.

Forgetting to finish feeding some animals during chore time or forgetting to close grain bin doors and gates caused many daily emergencies which we had to continually deal with. Emergencies and losses happened so often they became a normal daily experience, keeping my mother and I on edge.

Little did mother understand his real condition. Nor did the rest of the family. As with a jigsaw puzzle, many pieces have to come together before the real picture begins to take shape and comprehension comes into view.

This was true in my father's case. Clues to his condition appeared separately, divided by many years of time, so connecting the dots was difficult.

Southwestern Alberta has a climate that commands your attention, especially in the winter. Keeping in touch with weather reports is a daily must. Following these reports can become like a religion. Conditions can change in very short notice, from those balmy Chinook winds bringing a pleasant break to subzero temperatures, to a life threatening polar blizzard in a matter of a couple of hours.

Summertime yields its usual hot days which can give birth to severe thunderstorms. These can develop into even more dreaded severe hail storms. Hail storms are those ominous thunder heads that preclude massive amounts of damage to crops and gardens usually with complete destruction. Shingles on your roof can be damaged or destroyed and the windows in your house cracked or worse. As these storms move eastward forming dark ominous thunder heads after rising over the mountains, they can drop their moisture in the form of rain or hail. When the thunderhead is forming hail, the cloud becomes a medium grey. As the storm approaches a roar can be heard from the icy stones hitting surfaces and the air becomes icy cold. Seven years in a row we lost our crops and garden because of these kinds of storms. Our area was considered the worst hail belt in the world other than an area somewhere in Russia which had the same problem that our region had.

That seventh year we were not only hailed out but a tornado decided to put our house and farm buildings in its chosen path. We lost my father's grain field, the garden, and the strawberry patch; all wiped out including our raspberry patch which was close to coming into production. These fruits were our foundational food preserves during the winter months.

The tornado took the roof off our not very well-built house and destroyed several out buildings. Our dog was dropped somewhere in the grain field and blinded, but managed to find his way home by the sound of our voices calling his name. The chickens were scattered for undetermined distances but they too kept returning home for several days. Most did arrive back; however, the head count was never made the same. Two of our pigs were killed, several being injured by having an assortment of various lacerations.

My father, mother, and I managed to escape the wrath of this rarity of a storm for Alberta. There had been no history of such so watching for them was not a habit we had practiced. Mother had shared with me life experiences in North Carolina and watching for tornados was on that list. She had described to me in detail what a tornado could look like. Fortunately, that day the information she had relayed to me came forward into my consciousness, enabling me to draw to mother's attention what I was seeing. That probably saved our lives.

On this early August afternoon I had been out in the yard doing what comes naturally to country living. While I busied myself, I noticed thunderheads forming on the western mountain horizon. As I watched them developing and noticing something unusual which I had never seen before, a funnel cloud became part of the overall storm head. I called to Mother feeling the need to get her attention. I was relating in my mind her stories to what I was seeing. While we both were watching the funnel disappeared. Mother remained cautious by taking steps to put the fire out in the wood burning cook stove. She continued to verbally rattle off thoughts which were going through her mind regarding precautions to take during such an event. I listened to her chatter as this was a subject that lacked any depth of meaning to me, since Alberta had no history for these kinds of storms.

With the funnel cloud disappearing we let our guard down When the hailstorm hit with its fury we thought we were going to lose our kitchen windows. Even though Mother was only a few feet away she had to yell to my dad and me to communicate. The hailstones were causing a loud roar as they fell against surfaces. Fetching some bed pillows to hold against the window panes seemed to be the solution needed to protect the windows. Mother's window began to vibrate. Opening her window to allow the icy stones right into the room, in the process her pillow slipped allowing her to see circulating airborne debris outside. She made a fast mental connection in her mind, screaming to my Dad and me to get to the cellar. I followed quickly, and my father hesitated for a moment eventually following too. While crouched down in the cellar an unbelievable roar was taking place above us. Seeing the house lift off its footing and hang in mid air for a number of seconds then settling back down in its place, the roar ceased and complete stillness filled the air. As we climbed up from the cellar the first thing we saw was blue sky. The roof on the house was gone. Looking around, the interior of our home was now a soaking mess. My mother's piano was totally exposed to the elements; however, it did not seem to have water in the interior. We placed a sheet of plywood over it for protection from any further nasty elements.

Walking around outside, the ravages of the storm stared us in the face. We were anything but wealthy but now we had a lot less. One grain bin was completely destroyed and the other one was relocated about two hundred feet over into the neighbor's woods. The roof was off but was leaning against one side wall while remaining mostly intact. That grain bin was the one my father had put our dog in before the storm. We called and called our pet's name. Finally, we saw him running across the field toward the house but managed to collide with a fence post. Seeing that, we knew something was wrong. Approaching us by following the sound of our voices we could see that his eyes were swollen and completely turned a grayish white. Many months later his eyesight returned slightly, but never made a complete recovery.

The previous week I had finished sewing my dress for next year's school junior banquet. Anticipating my need for this banquet I had planned a sewing project while home during the summer months. While surveying the tornado's destruction I found my dress hanging on a branch in a thick wooded area. Upon retrieving the soaked garment, a big six inch rip on the side of the skirt was very evident. With no money for replacement, I mended the hole wearing it to the spring banquet anyway.

Tornados create some very interesting stories. Since we had our own experience and thank God we survived unharmed, others who have experienced them testify to the extraordinary as well. As it turned out my parents and I were the only living beings that weren't physically injured or killed during this tornado's touchdown. The pickup truck being parked next to the grain bin had fresh green leaves within the tightly closed cab while the bin was completely destroyed. My father's field plow was moved about twenty feet, which is astounding since they are made of heavy steel with very little surface to provide any kind of air lift. The utility trailer with its tailgate in a closed position had a board thrust between the tailgate and the body of the trailer. These stories seem unbelievable until they are witnessed first-hand.

As we walked around surveying the damages, our minds were in a state of shock. Taking in the scope of this sudden change in our farm environment was overwhelming. How were we ever going to recover from this disaster? How were we ever going to rebuild and replace what had been lost? The devastation was more than the mind wanted to deal with. My father had enough problems dealing with the routine of life, much less emergency situations, or solving problems that demanded in depth planning.

Hope showed up through the owner of the grocery store we often patronized. We were very grateful as he stayed on the recovery project until the roof was replaced. He was the only one in the community who offered any help. Our buildings and one other neighbor's property were affected by the storm. No one from our rural community stopped by to see if we were okay or how recovery was taking place. It wasn't until more light came on my father's condition that I began to understand why.

In a different community a church held a shower helping to replace linens and other household items that were destroyed by the storm. That act of kindness was so emotionally uplifting that it brought some renewed hope for survival. Presently, I have a wool filled patchwork quilt the ladies made for us. Every time I see or use their quilt I thank them in my mind for their kindness. Through these acts of kindness, hope began to take root again. Life was beginning to go forward with some mental relief. Perhaps life would still be manageable and mother would be alright when I left for school again in the fall.

Cold Alberta winters can present their own challenges. The greatest extreme I recall was in a January during a very long cold spell. For three weeks nighttime temperatures dropped to minus forty degrees rising minimally during daytime. One morning upon arising to meet the day, the sun was shining and the snow was melting off our roof thanks to that Chinook wind. (Those are warm air winds coming off the warm water current that flows up the west coast toward Alaska). However, that sunny warm air only lasted for a few hours. By four o'clock that afternoon the Arctic north winds sent temperatures back down to forty below, amounting to an eighty degree temperature change within a matter of a couple of hours.

Our house was only approachable by a dirt and rocky lane that connected with the county's no name road. This lane was fine for travel in the summer when conditions were dry. It was a different story when there was too much rain, or during spring thaws, and during those North Pole winter polar blizzards.

Staying out of the ditch during less than ideal driving conditions, required the skills of a brave and experienced driver. The clay dirt becomes soft and slippery like warm butter when it is wet. After a deep snow, or dealing with snow drifts, during spring thaws creating big mud holes, or heavy rains, the same type of driving skills are required. Lack of fear, determination, and the skills of a race car driver got you through. Studying your road conditions, starting your engine, then, psyching yourself up by pushing your gas pedal to the floor, and doing some wild steering, you hope you make it to the end of this half mile wild ride. There is one rule not to be broken, which is whatever you do don't stop till you reach the county road. Getting started again under those roads conditions would prove to be impossible. If you are a faint hearted driver it will not take long for that to change.

Victory would be celebrated by yelling, "We made it." Sometimes it would turn out to be an "OH NO," experience. That is when Dad would go and get his old Case tractor with its big lug wheels while you sat and waited to be extracted.

This story that Mother shared with me took place when I was a two year old. It is also a story that relates how Mother practiced her own faith. I had become very ill with a high fever of 105 lasting for three days and had stopped eating. She was now convinced that I was not going to survive. Doctors didn't have many answers either for a lot of illnesses. Also going to the doctor was a self pay system and people didn't have the means to go for medical help, and as a result self treatment was what everyone was accustomed to and relied on.

Mother had her own methods of dealing with illnesses. She had in her mind remedies for dealing with colds and flu. She had innately inherited this interest from her grandfather. However, my high fever had not responded to any of her treatments. Antibiotics were not developed as of yet so that remedy was not an option as a treatment. As her last resort she went to her cabinet and got this homemade poultice stuff that she had mixed together previously. It was something that she always kept on hand. This time she was desperate. Spreading a layer of this stuff in a cotton cloth, then wrapping it around my throat and holding it in place with her hands for two hours. She claimed that to be a turning point in my recovery. Soon I was eating again and my fever started to recede.

Heaven only knows how she made that mixture she called a poultice. A long time later I saw this brown sticky stuff wrapped in a cloth up in the cupboard where she kept it. I only know that she referred to it as a remedy for sore throats and colds.

She was convinced that God had answered her prayers and must have a special reason for my survival. Only God Himself knows the answer to that. I do know that Mother was a praying person and that a recovery came about. God tells us to make our requests known to Him and in faith believe that He will answer. This is a basic principle of faith God has given us to live by.

Anyone who has had experience or understands the explosiveness of gasoline or kerosene will comprehend the utter devastation that can result from a fuel explosion.

I was an ignorant five year old and had no understanding of the danger that I was about to create. Mother had no way of foreknowing the action that I was about to perform while she was pouring kerosene, from a larger container to a smaller one. I was sitting in the grass about two feet away from her and for some unknown reason I decided to pull out a match from my pants pocket and light it. As soon as the match flamed my mother screamed. I instantly knew I had done something wrong so I quickly blow the flame out. As an adult, the conclusion which I came to is that the flame of the match and the fumes of the fuel had not as yet mixed. However, a flame and fuel needs only an instant to mix and explode. I see an example of that every time my husband starts a campfire for our family. Every time he does, my mind goes back to that memory and I shudder. The outcome of this scene could have been utter devastation with severe burns and scaring for life, if we had survived.

I don't allow myself to think about what an awful outcome could have taken place. I prefer to think in terms of the grace of God protecting us from horrible accidents that might have been. I also prefer to think in terms of God having a greater plan for our lives than what we could envision for ourselves. Believing He preserves us in His mercy for this greater plan is an act of faith. A life lived out in faith, believing God is intimately involved with daily knowledge of our goings and comings because He loves us, is very comforting.

The proof of Christ's love was witnessed and recorded over two thousand years ago by those who were present in the Garden of Gethsemane at the time of His crucifixion. Every Easter we testify to that historically recorded event by our celebration of His death and resurrection. Through communion we are drawn to remember his devoted love and sacrifice made available to all mankind. By accepting His free gift of forgiveness, we prove our life of faith by allowing Him to direct our daily path. Christ said He voluntarily went to the cross so that we could have a more abundant life here on earth and eternal life with Him in the hereafter. Because Christ paid the ultimate sacrifice of giving His life for us, He declared there is no other way to heaven except through Him.

Whenever I go back in my thoughts to that day, I have to bow my spirit in thanksgiving, for the miracle of preservation for my life. My prayer,

"Lord, I don't want anything to be a part of my life that would discredit Your name." Of course, I know that is impossible to live in such a way to never discredit God's character. However, to not appreciate what He has done, is to not recognize the wholeness of a Power that exists whether we want to accept Him or not. Each day that I have lived, I see it as a gift allowed and a miracle of preservation. Disasters can happen and change life forever in the twinkling of an eye.

I acknowledge that bad things happen to good people and that fact cannot be denied. An act of faith is believing that there must be a purpose for these times as well. Personally experiencing difficult times is when I have grown into a greater understanding of spiritual principles. My priorities in life become much clearer.

Farm accidents usually are disastrous unless there is an awareness providing enough preventive measures to avoid such events. Mother continually worried about my father in this regard. In many situations he seemed to lack that awareness, at other times he seemed able to foresee and avoid risky situations.

Whenever I was at home I was assigned the job of, "Go check on your Dad." I felt so frustrated by the constant requests that one day I said to myself, "Why do I have to go and check on Dad? I'm the kid, they should be checking on me." At the time being about ten years old I knew Dad was accident prone. I was feeling very frustrated by his seeming ineptness. I felt like my mother and I were always trying to get my father to take responsibility for himself. As a child, you are expecting the father figure to behave like a responsible parent and seeing that lack, frustration takes hold in your spirit. I felt like I was helping my mother parent my father instead of him parenting me. A cloudy aura seemed to continually hang over our lives. At this stage of our lives neither my mother nor I had any inkling regarding the real problem we were dealing with.

The following story happened during my absence from home but was one Mother related to me. She had a strong inner pull to go and check on my father since she had not seen or heard any sign of him for awhile.

My father was out working in the forested area using his tractor to move some previously cut down logs. She walked through the sheep corrals but still did not see him. Proceeding further and continuing toward the creek, she saw the tractor resting on the slope of the creek bank. Checking further, she found my father pinned under the tractor wheel immersed in the cold spring water. Just how long he had been in this situation she apparently didn't know. In her fright she managed to drive the tractor up the bank, releasing him from under the wheel. Hypothermia had not affected him severely at the time of her discovery but he was just cold and wet.

How he managed to get himself in this situation, seemed to come from his inattentiveness. The position in which he had parked the tractor in relation to the creek bank and his own standing position, turned out to be a bad mix. Usually he would use some sort of a physical block to prevent an implement from rolling either direction when not being driven. Obviously, he had not used a block this time, allowing the tractor to roll backwards, somehow pinning him under the wheel.

A nerve-wracking habit my father practiced often in the winter time, kept anyone present on edge. To get his old Case tractor started in bitter cold temperatures, a fire would be built underneath to warm up the engine. It didn't matter that gasoline was in the gas tank, he would start the fire anyway. A pile of wood stacked underneath, and then a small amount of gasoline tossed onto the stacked pile with a lighted match giving the final touch with the usual whoooosh. The rising heat from the flame warmed the engine enough, enabling it to start. To the amazement of the onlooker, that tractor never went up in flames.

On another occasion mother related a story to me which had given her reason to worry in a different manner.

My parents had accumulated approximately a hundred head of hogs, more than what could be housed in the straw roofed barn. Since there were lots of large pine trees on the property that could offer animal shelter the herd was moved to this thick pine forested area. My father's morning chore routine included their feeding. All was going well until one day shortly after leaving, he returned to the house claiming that all the pigs were missing. Mother couldn't believe it. Being in a bit of a shock she went to investigate for herself. When going and checking the situation she found the whole herd right where they were supposed to be. She now had some big questions swirling around in her mind without any answers, leaving her mind in a confused state.

Even though shadows were clouding my emotional life during my early years I have some good memories of times spent with my father.

Winter evenings spent out in subzero weather on a moon lit night cause objects to become dark and indistinguishable in the nighttime darkness. That, contrasting with the moon's light shining on icy frosted snow, provides a picture that defies capture. Long moonlight shadows form silhouettes of nature's objects that are framed by the glistening subzero frozen snow which is caressed by the moon's soft touch of light. A picture that defies capture but becomes frozen in the memory bank's keepsakes.

These nighttime scenes become enhanced by each step you take when hearing the crispy crunch of frozen snow under your boots as they make the crackling sound of a large bowl of dry corn flakes. These sounds are winter's natural thermometer reminding you that very chilly conditions exist. The rhythm of the draft horse's hooves on the icy frozen snow creating that crunch sound adds a musical wonder to the wintery night. The big hay sled which they are pulling reminds you of the job you clothed yourself to do.

These scenes from winter nights I remember as a child while helping my father haul oat bundles or hay to the cattle. The cold winter weather of Alberta is something that you adjust to and learn to live with. Daylight time in the middle of the winter is very short. A lot of living takes place after darkness has arrived, presenting scenes that otherwise would be missed.

Remembering these childhood moonlight winter scenes motivated me to expose my own children to experience life on a moonlight night. As a result, I took our three kid siblings for a moonlight horseback ride at midnight in the middle of the winter. We saw memorable scenes never visible in daylight. The horses knew this was a different routine, displaying puzzled expressions on their faces as we tacked up. They were a bit skittish but good sports about their midnight adventure. Collapsing sheets of crusty snow under their feet kept them on edge with the spooky sounds causing to them to buckle their knees. These wintery moonlight scenes create a lasting imprint onto your memory that cameras can't capture although artists have tried. I feel grateful that as a family we were in a position to provide this experience for our children. Needless to say, I have a love nature that began as a child and that has not faded. Nature is one of God's prescribed tranquilizers taken from His own pharmacy.

Author with Jim and his favorite pet

Jim on a hunting adventure

Off-Roading in Southern California

My parents with our children and the remnants of their sheep herd

Go-Carting in a Big Red tributary

Mother and Grandma Nanny with our baby daughter log sitting in the berry patch eating blueberry sandwiches

With mother summer players cast standing in nature's theater

With Grandpa Garfield in front of his name-sake booth

My father's stooked field

Grandpa Garfield and Grandma Nanny
right after her massive stroke

My father with his pony and sheep

Our first camper with canvas cover

Camper with cover off

A harrowing event that replays itself out in my mind every now and then occurred during one of those winter evenings when I had gone with my father.

My father was driving his team of Clydesdales who were hitched up to the hay sled, (in the summer it has wheels so is called a hay wagon). We were entering the pine tree forested area where the hogs were kept giving them shelter from snowstorms, rain, and hot sunshine. This was also their feeding spot.

As we were entering the area, all of a sudden the horses became very excited, rearing and kicking in an uncontrolled manner. Immediately my father realized what was taking place, the newly purchased boar for breeding had escaped from his pen and was attacking the horses. My father managed to rein the horses out onto the snow covered trail which led to an open field. Reining in the horses enough to dodge trees we made it to openness. However, that boar would not give up. He tried to jump into the hay wagon then went back to lunging against the horses' flanks. This porker kept repeating this action. Finally, Dad was able to rein the horses out into full openness and let the horses go full speed, making very large circles in the deep snow. Fortunately that boar tired before the horses did. Relieved, we returned to the farm buildings. Dad announced that pig was going to market next week. We were all shocked at the aggressive behavior. My father had been in his pen for feeding. There had never been any sign of vicious aggression until that drama took place.

Mother managed to purchase a half section of land about eight miles away from our home site. My parents used that land for pasturing their accumulated herd of cattle. During the winter months the cattle were wintered at our home property. During the summer months these bovine critters were moved to the pastureland.

Cattle round up and moving day was a time I got to spend helping my father. I realize now that routine was something that he could handle pretty well without any huge glitch. At that time of my life I was just helping my father with a job that had to be done with no other thoughts going through my mind.

The day would start by tacking up our horses, equipping ourselves with attire appropriate for the job, and checking the day's weather conditions. Lunch was made from whatever was available, and then put into a cloth sack along with the day's equipment tied to the saddle with those leather laces in preparation for a day that was sure to be long before it ever got around to ending. There would be a full day of saddle time.

The actual roundup process started with the aid of a couple of border collies which we had for moving sheep. Cows that have no intention of going anywhere need some help bringing about a mental change. Communicating your plan involves using collies, some mechanical prods, a bit of yelling, and horse maneuvering. Changing the minds of dozens of cows at the same time takes a lot of energy, but eventually they get the idea and the roundup is organized enough to begin the trek.

Moving down country roads with this fleshy mass involves watching out for traffic. Usually enough dust rises to be easily spotted far enough away for a driver to become aware that livestock is blocking the road. One rider goes in the lead to warn approaching traffic and drivers usually responded with courtesy, until a passage is completed.

Finally arriving at the new pasture and hardly being through the entrance gate, those hungry beasts would start devouring the newly discovered fresh green grass. With our mission accomplished returning would go a lot faster and cleaner after following behind in the kicked up dust as the cattle walked. By the time the return trip was completed, we were covered with dust and dirt, the horses were exhausted, the dogs had enough dog work for a week, and we were ready to be out of the saddle.

My saddle seat was hard with absolutely no padding giving any kind of comfort. Mine was an old bronc one from my father's rodeo days. These weren't meant for sitting in more than ten seconds, which was rodeo success time but definitely not for endless hours. After dismounting is when your body lets you know how much abuse it received throughout the day's ride. That bowlegged cowboy appearance is a fully felt reality. Standing up straight on level ground after long saddle hours trying to realign all of your body parts gives full comprehension to that cowboy gait.

This experience I recall with a sense of humor, laughing to myself because of its rarity. Life's unexpected surprises sometimes bring us laughs after the incident but not during the occasion. This was one of those times.

My mother's father gave my mother the use of a half section of land located about fifteen miles away from our home farm. This land was covered with a lot of northern climate willows that grow well in semi-wet soil but provided us with great cattle grazing during the warm weather seasons. With the use of this property we now had close to a thousand acres to manage through crop production and pasturing.

A number of weeks had passed since we had done a cattle drive to this property. It was time to make a salt delivery, do a head count, and check for health issues. This was a herd maintenance routine that was required periodically.

My father, mother, and I embarked on this trip in our old model T car. These were our pre-jeep days. We arrived at the pasture land without a hitch. My father called the cattle with his big voice which they would recognize as a salt block delivery being left for them. We stood around counting the ones that showed up. After a time the count amounted to the same as the original. Some summers there were cattle rustling problems losing a dozen or so, losses that were hard to take. Mother with her veterinarian's eye would also do her observing, watching for health problems and giving a general inspection before we would decide to depart.

Upon returning to the car, my father started up the engine and put it in gear, but the car did not move. Repeating this act a few times the nervous conclusion was made that the transmission was not going to engage. With one more try, he discovered that the reverse gear worked while none of the other positions did. With no other choice to be made my father shifted into reverse and started driving backwards. Reversing down those country roads wasn't too bad until we reached our small town. Going backwards down the big foothill south of town my father was able to manage it. Reversing through main street was embarrassing but even that went quite well as very little traffic was on the move and not seeing anyone we knew helped to ease the embarrassment factor. Sitting in the twisted position, my father complained of a tired neck having had to look out the rear window for that length of time. Best of all, we didn't have to walk those fifteen miles home.

The thunderstorms, with all their destruction which occurred so continuously, became something we learned to dread. Research on this massive problem was being done by a provincial government sponsored program. My mother participated in the research project by collecting different sized hailstones by placing them in the freezer, dating, and timing the storm until an agent would come and collect her data.

Eventually the research resulted in a seeding method. As these storms formed and rose over the mountains, airplanes would fly under the clouds seeding them with the chemical silver iodide, to prevent ice from forming. This seeding method relieved the potential power, lessening the damage these storms could cause, however, their impact was always a threat and dreaded.

During those times it was hard for my parents to maintain hope for the future. Livestock feed would be in short supply and our garden would be wiped out. How were we going to eat and have food on the table?

Many of those devastating storms have left visual pictures in my mind. One of those storms left a different awareness that none of the others left. The tornado storm placed itself in number one position in severity; this one comes in at number two.

My mother and I had gone to town for the day, a distance of thirty miles one way. We probably went for farm supplies, etc. never doing mother-daughter shopping since there was never any money for that. Only the very necessary supplies would ever be purchased. Difficult weather and road conditions purposed my mother to eventually buy a Willy's Jeep. They could go anywhere under almost any condition. However, on this day there was no jeep to help us out.

As mother and I were returning home from town we could see thunderclouds rising rapidly over the Rockies in the west. As mother was driving the storm moved off to our right missing the highway we were traveling on. However, this storm was broad enough to pass over our farm area just before we drove into the vicinity leaving a measurable depth of hailstones as an icy ground cover. About two miles from home our vehicle could not go any further, being unable to push through the depth of the hailstones. There we sat thinking. Within a short period of time mother said, "We are walking home". Opening the car doors we stepped out into those icy cold hailstones and walked home. Our freezing feet were definitely a motivation to keep moving.

A distinguishing memory I have of this storm's aftermath was the pungency produced from mother's onion patch, filling the air with a strong onion aroma drifting and lofting in the air a mile away. It was unbelievable that a row of pulverized onions could emanate such far reaching pungency.

Another aspect of those dreaded thunderstorms were the electrical charges set off in our house due to improper grounding of the electrical system. My father was not one to understand how electricity works or how it was to be properly installed, which caused some frightening situations. Any electrician who was hired was just someone who went by that name. That did not mean they knew what they were doing but knew how to string wires from point A to point B. Plugging in your appliance and also having it work spelled success. My parents hired them because they didn't charge much and were affordable. Any construction or repairs that were done by these self proclaimed skilled workmen laid the foundation for badly needed permits and licensing requirements. Anything more than routine was beyond my father's skill level so outside help came from a resource list of people compiled by my mother.

The house's main electrical box was inside the front door high on the wall. Opening and stepping through the front door places you in the kitchen. Many times during a thunderstorm with lightening doing its intense flashing, electrical power surges would hit the power box sending a flash across the room to the kitchen sink. Apparently this was happening because the electrical system had not been grounded properly while the kitchen faucets being filled with water were providing a ground.

We learned to avoid the kitchen area when the air was so turbulent.

On another occasion during such an electrically charged storm, we made the mistake of leaving the sitting room window and bedroom window open at the same time. Fortunately, no one was in the path of the electrical surge from the lighting flash as it came in the sitting room window and went out the other. The bedroom closet became our refuge during those stormy times being the only place where we felt any safety. After the tornado episode even that was questionable.

A regular occurrence involved our phone system which would be decommissioned for several days at a time in a storm's aftermath. Our telephone lines were all above ground and primitive, being exposed to the electrical charges from lightening causing the entire system to be overwhelmed. That would end all communication for several days with anyone in the community or the outside world.

Until the telephone company got around to repairing the system, temporary makeshift repairs were a task undertaken by ourselves. After a storm and high winds had passed through, many telephone poles would either be blown down or badly leaned over. The telephone wires would be sagging so badly they would be touching the ground interrupting the service. Wanting to communicate with anyone and the phone company had not shown up, the temporary repairs were yours to do. Many times we have propped up poles and stretched the wire off the ground in order to reconnect the service.

In today's digital world these conditions are difficult to imagine or relate to and are maybe even humorous.

Establishing Life in the River Valley

THE EXPECTATION FOR MARRIED LIFE was for a basic beginning during The Great Depression. Progress and changes would be slow to develop. Country life would have an influence on the kinds of wedding gifts a couple would receive. A milk cow for a supply of milk, chickens would provide meat and eggs for the table as well as grocery money when sold at the local creamery. Maybe a couple of beef cows or pigs would be on the gift list. To have that kind of a start for a newly married couple would be foundational, giving some hope for a progressive and successful future. Heirlooms and personally crafted finery gifts would be on the list by the generosity of family and friends. Cast-offs were also a norm.

My father had been promised a quarter section of land by his father but not given official ownership. These one hundred sixty five acres were adjacent to his father's Three Bar Cattle Ranch. This plot of land was bordered on the eastern edge by The Three Bar Ranch and by Big Red on the western side. This plot of land established the direction my of parent's married life. Their roots were being planted for years to come. This seemed to be the natural direction for them to take, and so it was. This river land became their home.

My parent's two bedroom primitive cabin was built on a rocky knoll which had been created by Big Red during an earlier era of the river. Over time, Big Red had carved out this whole valley lying between the two foothill ranges. The current water flow hugged the western foothill range, eliminating this knoll from its path. Small ridges and springs that bubbled up through the earth's surface created a buffer zone between their building site and the current river bed.

Men had come together to help build this basic structure. Perhaps my Dad's father and his hired men, along with a couple of neighbors got together for the construction project. I was never privy to this aspect of their married life's beginning. Living daily life and its stresses seemed to get in the way of remembering to ask for such information.

The foundation of the two room structure was the rocky river bed which had been built up over the millennial of time. Rocks being tumbled over each other by the rapid flowing mountain stream rounded off any rough edges enabling the stones to tightly fit together to form a solid foundation for their cabin. Long logs laid over these solidly packed river stones became the cabin's foundation.

A shallow well was dug before construction of the cabin began. The water table was shallow eliminating the need for a lot of depth through this compacted football sized river stone. Digging through those stones was no small feat. Generally a horse drawn fresno scoop was the tool used for excavation.

This well would be under the cabin's floor to fulfill water needs after a hand worked lift pump was installed through the washroom floor. This would guarantee a ready supply of water for daily needs. The well head was then covered with loosely laid short boards. During spring thaws or times of heavy rains the well's water level would rise right along with Big Red. When Big Red rose to flood level so would the well's water, sometimes flooding the crawl space under the cabin making it unfit for drinking. This space allowed for well inspection and provided limited storage. Eventually this area became a root cellar.

We never trusted this well for our drinking water due to its shallowness. Our drinking water was carried by hand in a water bucket from one of those bubbling fresh water springs about a quarter mile away. When Big

Red flooded we hauled our drinking water from my mother's parents. Big Red didn't overflow its banks that often so transporting water would be short term.

    The first twelve years of my parent's marriage were spent in this two room cabin before an addition was built, and that was never finished. One room was their bedroom with a small closet; the second was organized with the shared space idea. A breakfast nook with a small window over the table and a built in wall- cabinet filled one corner of the room. The wood burning cook stove and space heater shared the rest of the room with a built in wood box, wash room for washing your hands etc, small sitting area with a large boot box that swallowed any remaining area. Because of the box's size we could also use it as a sleeping cot. Mother also had a baker's cabinet under the second window close to the old cook stove.

    Coal oil lamps that gave off as much light as a candle provided night time lighting. We had one lamp so a lot of darkness existed in every corner of the room. Reading was difficult so we did not do much of that unless you held your page within a foot of the lamp. Sometimes mother would light the kerosene lamp with mantles which provided much more light for reading. The problem with that lamp was that it needed mantles which cost money so it was rarely used. When that lamp was burning was when Mother would read aloud to us the funnies from the newspaper publications.

    During construction of the cabin, wood shavings and saw dust were used for insulation in the walls. The weight of the shaving or saw-dust would settle eliminating any protection from cold air filtering through the boards. The top twenty four inches of the wall literally had no insulating factor where warm air would rise but also have the greatest heat loss. By today's standards the R factor would be considered zero. My mother wall-papered with heavy brown utility paper to cut down on wind drafts and snow that blew between the cracks of the boards.

Since there was no basement under this cabin but a deep bed of river rock, straw was piled around the outside base of the house to help keep those cold floors warmer in the winter. Logs laying on stones allowed for too much cold air circulation under the wood planking floors. Freezing temperatures in the root cellar was a concern as well. The winter cold had a way of making its presence continuously felt, with little reprieve.

Field mice had a great time in our house with an open foundation. They had a ready entrance whenever they wished. There was an ongoing battle between nature and our family, never seeming to take a break. In my mind, I can see mother stepping on top of some loose floor linoleum to squash some mice frolicking underneath. No wonder I have a phobia against the not so nice little critters. We had more field mice than all the farm cats could catch.

That root cellar became my mother's storage room for the hundreds of jars of canned fruits she would preserve each autumn season. These became a staple for our family's diet during the winter months. These fruits would come from the summer street markets in Calgary, when my parents would be in the city for livestock auction days. With the hailstorms continuously wiping out her garden another food source had to be found. My mother was very resourceful and always looking for a new idea.

Besides the two room cabin, these men also built a small log barn topped with straw blown on at thrashing time, providing a roof. No plank flooring but a dirt base gave the basics for this simple structure. When the snow melted or the rain came down heavily a leaking roof was an understatement. Straw has zero water repellency.

This basic structure of a barn and the two room cabin were the beginnings of my parent's married life.

Married life seemed to be going forward in slow motion. Mother's parents had given them some chickens, a cow and a pig. My father had a horse and a model T car plus a few head of Hereford cattle he had accumulated while working for his father on The Ranch. My father and his father apparently had this arrangement for employment with livestock as a paycheck. Going to work was convenient, seemed to be an ideal arrangement, and was the continuation of a long term prior agreement.

My father's parents were living across the road with their buildings in full view of ours. They were our closest neighbor. The distance between us was about a country mile; far enough away that neither we nor they could look into each other's windows and not have privacy. The remarkable factor regarding this close proximity to my grandparent's property is that I never met them. As I rethink life in this River Valley this fact seems too far-fetched to be true. However, living this situation out created many foggy and confusing days that never seemed to have a solution or an end.

While as a child, apparently around the age of six, my father was helping ranch hands build some fences on The Ranch. Apparently an accident occurred when my father was supporting a fence post while a hired man tried to pound it into the ground. While holding the post the maul missed the post hitting my father on the head. The force of the maul knocked him unconscious and then into a semiconscious state, a condition that remained for about three days. Information regarding this incident was very sketchy. When my father came out of his coma, his parents probably thought t he was now okay and they would have him back. Life could go on as normal. However, I now believe that they were unable to make any connection between the accident and any developing behavioral symptoms and unrecognized the long term consequences of this accident.

Mother related that story to me as a five year old child regarding my father's accident. She only made reference to that incident once and I never heard anyone else make reference to it at any other time. At the time it was just an "OH" statement which meant I heard the story but somehow it became part of my long term memory. I was too young at the time to decipher or attach any meaning to what she was telling me.

Selma J. Stroebel

Not only did I not understand, neither did she grasp the scope of what she was really sharing nor neither did my father's family grasp the depth of the accident's effect on my father. The gap of comprehending was Grand Canyon sized on the part of all involved. Fortunately, my mind had remembered those shared details but connecting any dots would take a lifetime. In light of how little this accident was ever referred to, I'm wondering what ever made my mother mention it to me in the first place and how did she find out about it. Obviously, my father had told her but had probably downplayed the accident in his own mind and it seemed so did everyone else.

My Dad's father had managed to amass about two thousand acres of land and a five hundred-head herd of purebred Hereford cattle. He also had dozens of draft horses plus numerous saddle horses. He had supplied cattle for the annual Calgary Stampede and was a provider of breeding stock for the prestigious Diamond Bar Ranch in southern California. Apparently his breeding bulls were in high demand. These figures and information I picked up through conversations which I was a witness to.

All of this livestock was provided for through grazing land and crop production acreages on these two thousand acres of property. After my father's parents passed away, a paper record revealed an appraisal he had prepared of all his property's worth. In nineteen hundred and nineteen this appraisal showed an evaluation of approximately one hundred thousand dollars. He was a very wealthy man for his time.

Being gregarious and politically minded, involving themselves with provincial issues, and the importance of social status, would describe my father's family's personalities.

It is difficult to put this following incident in a relational context that makes any sense.

Mother related to me that her father-in-law was shipping a load of cattle to market. At this point, family relations still seemed to be intact but fragile. My mother made a request for an apple for his three year old grandson when he returned from making this shipment. I was not on the scene as of yet so no request was made for me. He did bring an apple home for his grandson, but he also charged my mother for it. It was certainly his privilege to charge mother for the apple, however, a little generosity displayed would have convinced my mother that he really did value his grandson. In light of his wealth, maybe even a bag of apples would have been a nice gesture.

When I think of mother's shared story, I am challenged by our human value systems that can be so misplaced. My mind goes to the Easter story of Christ's sacrifice and His extreme suffering on the cross so that you and I can have a more abundant life, more than what we are able to choose for ourselves. Man lost that relationship with our Heavenly Father due to the sin that entered into the Garden of Eden through Eve, forever creating a relationship problem. Christ became an example of selflessness to restore that relationship between God and man. Comparing the man who clung to his pennies unable to share an apple with his own flesh and blood, with the One who sacrificed Himself on the cross so that we may live forever with Him if we choose to follow His footsteps, challenges our value system. This comparison has been a huge lesson for me creating the personal goal of trying to chose in life that which is truly important as a priority.

Shortly after this load of cattle was shipped, my father was informed that he would no longer be needed on The Ranch. He had left for work as usual one morning but returned home soon after. His father stated that the cattle herd was being reduced in number and that he would no longer be needed. This came as a surprise to my father and a shock to my mother. No forewarning or even a hint given to prepare my parents for this big change so that they could plan accordingly. My father had not been privy to any of the decision making process. The compensation my father received for his time spent working at The Ranch, were a few head of Hereford and a pair of draft horses he called Dick and Stub.

These horses were a part of our family for many years. As a child, I remember going out with my father and helping with the harnessing of these monsters. After the harnessing was completed and they were hooked up to the wagon, I got to ride on their backs.

This employment termination on the part of my father by his father was the first time that my parents were completely on their own. Mother describes this time in their lives as, "Nobody understood how poor we were". She stated that one winter the only money which they had in the house was one dime. She was afraid to spend it in case my father would need an aspirin for his headaches, which he would get often. They would be able to go to the druggist and buy only one pill. Druggists would listen to your symptoms then tell you what you needed. It was an often practiced system at the time, seeking medical help through the advice of the druggist since going to the doctor cost money and most people didn't have that.

Whatever happened between my father and his family was never discussed. There was a mystery which seemed to hang in the air. Family communication with his parents became nonexistent. Even though they lived across the road from us and their house was in full view of ours, as their granddaughter I never met them. Never a phone call, nor remembering birthdays, no gatherings at Christmastime either. Nothing was ever acknowledged or a visit to our home made. To me they were total strangers. My father never made a statement like, "Today let's go and visit Grandma and Grandpa." I don't know if he ever visited his parents on his own or not.

Without casual conversation and communication between family members the ability to comprehend reality becomes nonexistent. Nothing becomes solved but only magnified in the minds of those involved. What becomes magnified after awhile becomes truth. This was the situation I believe was happening in this family.

My parent's neighbor who was not afraid to speak of life the way he saw it, told my mother that my father's family were claiming that, "She was driving my father crazy." This was a wonderful rumor to have going around in a small town and country environment regarding your family life. This was a tough rumor to live down as a growing girl.

I knew that my father had a problem but I was totally clueless in my ability to understand him. I knew that my mother tried to get him to be responsible in working out our daily farm life. I also certainly knew that my mother was not driving him crazy. She deserved a lot more credit than that and it hurt so much to hear these false accusations. This talented and intelligent woman was working so hard to provide for a family under such difficult circumstances. She certainly was not responsible for driving my father crazy.

Informal communication had broken down to such a low level that it no longer existed. A method for thought exchange was of the formal kind. Communication between the two families was via a letter from an attorney or a personal letter delivered by mail. One day I came across a letter my father had received from his father, sometime in the distant past, asking for permission to drive across the corner of our land for some minor purpose of which I don't remember. This letter was a reflection of the cold relationship which existed between the two families, especially between father and son with no understandable explanation.

The second very unsettling formal communication my parents received came from an attorney with its jaw dropping content. One could only ask yourself, "WHY?"

The contents of this official legal affidavit were a direct order to move off the property and this task had to be accomplished within three days. Where were we going to go? How can you move all your livestock, your machinery, and household items in three days? That would be an impossible task, even if you knew where you were going. What legal recourse could be taken since my father's father had never issued a title for the property? Were they really willing to take our home away from us?

Selma J. Stroebel

I was thirteen years old that summer. I was told to go out and start taking down the fence around our house. I started to work on that project by myself for awhile until my mother called informing me that we were all going to town.

I didn't realize until later, what my mother had decided to do. She stated that she wanted to go and talk to their attorney. Entering his office and stating her reasons, he was firm in his demands. Walking out of his office he repeated, "Remember you have three days." I believe it was at that moment when my mother decided to hire her own attorney. Seeing that my father had no fight in his spirit, she had no choice.

The next town over my mother found an attorney who listened to this unbelievable story. He was willing to take her case. He could hardly believe what his ears were hearing. Her decision was to counter sue for defamation of character.

Upon returning home, mother heard her in law's phone ring. Being that the phone system was a seven family community service line, anyone could listen in on a conversation, learning the latest news in the community. Mother listened in on their call. The calling party was their attorney stating that he wished to have them come for a consultation as there was a change in their case that needed to be discussed. Obviously, mother's attorney had informed their attorney that there was going to be a counter suit.

A defamation of character suit could become very messy. Their public image would be tarnished and maybe that would be something they would want to avoid. No more communication was received from their attorney. When my grandfather passed away, a title to the land was finally granted to my father.

All legal action was immediately dropped. In time, I believe I was able to understand some reasons behind this legal action. Putting together puzzle pieces to create an understandable picture has taken a tremendous amount of emotional energy. Piecing together tidbits of information has been a slow process as they were distanced apart by many years.

Mother had been affected in a profound way. My father was not showing interest in the family's well being. It was becoming more apparent that he had some psychological dysfunctions going on that seemed to be periodic. He had sold the same bull, to two different people, and had forgotten that he had done so. He could have been in trouble with the law over that one, but it did get straightened out. Spending money which they didn't have, or being unable to account for money which he was supposed to have, was not making sense.

In the meantime, Mother was not receiving the emotional support which is expected from a spouse. With all of the stress in mother's life she was becoming a very unhappy person. Conflict between them was a constant ongoing war. She was trying so hard to make life work while he carried on with his chore routines, avoiding anything that involved extra thinking or conflict.

Getting an Education

Eagle Valley School---First Grade

SCHOOLING WAS A NON-TRADITIONAL experience. Living seven miles from our country school was always an adventure just to get there. No school buses in our area, so horseback was the method.

I was the youngest student, seven years of age, which came from our direction. My brother and I lived the farthest distance away while all of the other students lived varying distances, but closer than us. Along the way we would join up with other kids, all boys older than me, who rode their horses as well.

That sounds romantic to the ears of students today who must ride a school bus or with their parents who are ready and waiting to pick them up a block from the school's front door. Not much walking to keep the body fit. The comfort of a vehicle when the weather is inclement is a nice luxury. On horseback you are exposed to all of the elements of nature whether it is sunshine, rain, or the extreme cold of mid-winter. Using excuses to not attend school because of bad weather will not work for very long. Mother would bundle me with all of the warm clothing she could muster up during mid winter, for the hour and a half ride. The only things exposed on my body were two eye holes in a face mask. Protecting the skin from frost bite was a very real factor.

Living that experience demanded a determination to keep up with all the other riders. A girl tagging along was just that, a girl tagging along. If they decided to have their horses go full speed ahead I had to do the same.

I would hang onto my horse's mane; lay as flat as possible on his neck, then hope to survive it all. Survive I always did without much thought of either success or failure. I was pretty neutral about the way I felt and never was intimidated by being the youngest and only girl.

Arriving, we housed our horses in the school barn with all of the other student's horses. I guess the horses got along as I was not aware of any barn problems during the day. My brother was the one who stalled and managed the horse details.

The return home was a reverse in activity from the morning. My brother and I would lose riders the further we rode toward home. Eventually we would be by ourselves continuing on with our horses ready for a much slower pace. Boys like to race each other so the horses were ready to have that competition end.

We had three tributaries of Big Red to ford before arriving back home. One spot had formed a deep water pool as a result of Big Red's high water flow earlier in the season. I was totally unaware and unprepared for what my horse was about to do. He walked out into the deeper depth of the water drinking as he walked. Suddenly he started pawing the water while my response was this is a lot of fun until he laid down in the water. Now I'm in water up to my chest with my saddle totally under water. I managed to dismount, get out of the water and then watch my horse recover from his antics. I learned that a horse will do that when they want to cool off. I guess my horse was a lot warmer than I was aware of. In the meantime my brother had a good laugh.

I didn't do all that well academically during my first grade year. When I look back I think I probably needed a nap before school started. The initial energy of the day was already used up with little still available for math and reading.

Our schoolhouse was one of those one room things that had all nine grades within one room. The heating system was a great big wood and coal furnace that occupied a quarter of the rear of the class room. The fire starters were early arrival students who lived nearby and compensated for having a warm enough room that you did not have to wear a jacket during class time.

Country school teachers were usually young single women who did not remain single long, usually marrying a local bachelor. Living quarters were provided by an attached rustic suite at the rear of the schoolhouse. Rustic meant there would be no indoor plumbing or electricity. The water supply would be from the school yard well. Social life for them would be through social engagements with the local people however, there was a strict conduct code which they were expected to comply with. The conduct code requirement included no smoking, drinking, or going to the local licensed pub. The pub, never open on Sundays, required women to be escorted by a male.

Leaving Eagle Valley/ Going to Sundre

Education taking place in a one room school seemed like a big negative to many, but not to me. The younger children learned from the upper grades about subject matter and expectations that were going to be required in the following year. This was actually an advantage. A first grader would be learning about what it would be like to be a second grader. This seemed to be an advantage rather than a disadvantage.

Country school education was coming to a close and giving way to the composite school system. Country schools were closing and students were going to be bused to the nearest incorporated town. Within a three year period the whole system would became centralized.

Since the centralized system was becoming the new plan for student education, Mother made the decision that my brother and I were going to transfer starting with my second year. She was not going to wait for the centralized system to be fully implemented as she had not been impressed with my first grade teacher.

There existed a big problem regarding that decision; transportation for getting to school. There would be no bus service coming our direction as my brother and I were the only kids on the north side of town and too far out for the bus to come our way. The school bus would pick up those who lived on the highway but nowhere else. It was your job to get to the highway, regardless of where you lived. Deep snow drifts along with the severe winter weather would make the roads impassable for my parents. Our currently owned vehicles would not be able to move through such conditions. Having the job of driving to town daily was something my parents would not be able manage. It would literally be an impossible task for them to routinely accomplish driving twenty miles twice daily.

Mother came up with a different plan. She rented a cottage in town and persuaded my grandmother to live with us kids during the school week. My grandmother obliged by consenting to live with my brother and me until my grandfather retired from his provincial employment eighteen months later.

Little did I know that I would be experiencing a lot of changes in my future education and that this was only the beginning. As it turned out, my first grade year was the only year in which I lived at home to attend school. My second grade year started a whole new approach to getting an education.

Life for the family had become deeply entrenched on this river land. Making changes to accommodate getting an education seemed to be elusive and relocating the family was out of the question for many practical reasons. The idea of renting this cottage located only a few blocks from school seemed to be the answer mother was looking for. This would mean that us kids would be away from home everyday living with our grandmother but would be home with our parents on the weekends.

Now living in town in the rented cottage with my grandmother, the weather still warm, my brother and I were adjusting by meeting and making new friends. Fall had come and the new school was under way. We could ride our bikes around town spending our leisure time the way we wanted. This was a new life for us and we liked it.

Before long the warm weather ended making way for winter to arrive coming in mid-fall in Alberta. Just getting to town in order to stay the week, created new memories and experiences with the winter weather.

Dad would harness up his Clydesdales hooking them up to the sleigh which had been converted from the utility wagon. The sleigh now being outfitted with runners to easily glide over any depth of snow was always an open air mode of transportation. The newly converted sleigh glided easily along like traveling with the wind at your back with the large boned and heavy muscled team of Clydesdales effortlessly pulling the sleigh through the deep snow. This winter scene is a reminder of Norman Rockwell artistry.

Preparation for this long open air frigid ride with icy cold winds blowing in your face penetrating your heavy outdoor winter attire, required some serious preparation. Mother prepared for these threatening conditions by heating field stones for several hours in the wood burning stove's oven. Leaving them there for several hours assured her these stones were thoroughly warmed and would provide heat during the number of hours the sleigh trip would take. Wrapping them in newspaper and tying with twine she would then place them at our feet wrapping our entire body with an extra layer of wool blankets. With those warm stones placed inside those wool blankets by our feet we were able to stay comfortably warm for the long, frigid, two-hour sleigh ride. My father still had the return trip to make so he had double time.

Living in our rented one bedroom cottage with my grandmother lasted for a year and a half. Half way through my third grade year Grandpa Garfield retired from his government job. With a reunion trip planned for visiting family back in North Carolina, Grandma's time of living with us came to an end. This was a long over-due family reunion being nearly thirty years since their last visit.

Mother let our rented cottage go. I went to live with my aunt's sister staying there for three weeks. I was now nine years old. My brother, now fourteen, went to live with his friend's family.

The path we would be taking to get our education was becoming cast in stone. Predetermined by our home's location, being too far away for any kind of services that are taken for granted today, just didn't exist. The farm roots my parents had established would not be easy to transplant. Mother had verbalized the desire to purchase land closer to town, however, she knew that would never become a reality. That kind of move would require more of a change than my father would ever be able to accept.

As our school years progressed my mother's concern about the lack of family togetherness was understandable. The continuing inconvenience was definitely disrupting our daily family life. Time together was now limited to weekends and summer vacation and that slipped by quickly.

Living with other families:

Being away from home for school life gave me a reprieve from my own family's hectic life, my mother's understandable frustrations, and the conflict which existed between my parents.

I experienced other's lives in a unique way. Being able to be a daily observer in such an intimate way gives you a glimpse of how others organize their time, how they carry out their responsibilities, their methods of articulating in communication with each other, the talents they possess, and what they truly value. It also showed how the children used their recreation time and how the families related to each other. The family dynamics were mostly healthy in all the families with whom I lived. Mother had been careful in choosing the homes in which I would stay.

Living away from home was now extending into my fourth grade year. I was now living with a farm family with the advantage of being on the school bus route. Three siblings: a teenage boy, a girl a year older than me, and another girl a couple years younger; plus the parents composed this mixture of personalities.

The outstanding factor in this family was the musical ability of the middle daughter. She was a rare specimen with an abundance of talent, both instrumentally and vocally. Her instrument was the piano and was very accomplished at a young age. Her ability was to listen to a new piece of music one time through, then go sit down to her piano and play the whole piece from ear. The voice which she possessed was another gift beyond belief. As a seventh grader, she sang for concerts with a mature, professional voice without having had voice lessons and eventually singing opera for the Vancouver Opera House, in British Columbia.

While living in this household my relationship with her held some tension. Immaturity focuses on what we have and are proud of, or what we don't have and feeling intimidated by our lack of whatever it is. Bottom line in this situation was she had the talent and I didn't have much musical ability. She delighted in reminding me of my lack. In other aspects of our friendship we got along fine.

I liked the structure this family lived by and resided with this family for two years. However, no matter how much you feel comfortable with others on their turf, you know that this not your family. They know it too. You are present both in body and spirit, but you are never a real member of their unit. You learn how to blend into the pack as well as you can.

Another experience I had was living with an elderly lady who also lived on the same bus route. I had never met this lady before living with her. She was a total stranger to me but apparently she and my mother were acquainted. Our first meeting was the first night in which I stayed with her.

Making a wonderful warm and tasty meal every night, I was impressed with the fare which she served. I knew she had the time to cook and mother didn't. Before placing any food on my plate it would first be warmed in her oven. I had never seen that done before and I mentally took note thinking that was different and a nice way to live.

Time living with this lady was a short span of about a month. I believe providing for a kid at her elderly age became too much of a chore for her to continue with this arrangement. Again, I moved on to another home but left with favorable thoughts regarding my time spent with her. Unfortunately, I probably never thanked her for her kindness. Kids are not always thoughtful and I was probably guilty of that.

Starting my sixth grade year I found myself living with a Norwegian family who were recent immigrants from Norway and were unable to speak any English. They had moved into this foothills community to be near other family members who had come to the region earlier. How my mother made contact with them was another question I never asked.

Two girls were a part of this family's unit; one was my age, and the other a couple years younger. We had some interesting times trying to communicate. Kids are resourceful they just find a way. During the two years of living with them I picked up some Norwegian and could understand more from their conversation than I could speak.

Another home where I spent some time was with an older couple. They lived a couple of blocks from school so that was very convenient for me and I liked that. However, his wife had the habit of going to bed early making me feel very uncomfortable with actions and comments which the husband made. Mother was very astute. When I mentioned my uneasy feeling, that was the last week I stayed with them. My time with them lasted three weeks.

Between the time of finishing my third grade year while living with my grandmother and completing eighth grade, I had lived in six different settings. That was an education of a different kind. You are present in their environment but never a real participant. You are always the extra one, the one they remember to include at the last minute, like, "Oh yes we need to include ----," in any event, chore, or their family time together. Everyone was as considerate as they could be but the emotion of always being the extra one was always present in my mind.

Time spent living at home with my parents under their roof amounted to a lot less time than living with others under their rooves. Being home for weekends, a week at Christmas and Easter, plus two months in the summer, is not much family time for a kid that is ten years old or as an early teenager. Our absence as kids was something that bothered my mother very much. Without the cooperation of my father, her options were very limited. By the time my brother finished tenth grade, he left home.

Prairie High School at Three Hills, Alberta

Mother was concerned for her teenage daughter and the kind of supervision which she felt I needed. Little time spent at home plus her absence of personal parenting caused her to consider a totally different direction for my education. She was afraid that as a teenager I would be too unsupervised and trouble could follow. Free time for a teenager with little supervision and growing outside influences was a bad mix she refused to accept.

I walked into the house one late summer day with mother turning to me and announcing "You have been accepted at Prairie Bible Institute High School." No application had been filled out; only a phone call made to the school's office and my acceptance was made over the phone. I knew very little about the school so I didn't have negative or positive feelings. I did know that I would be away from home a lot more than before. This was a boarding school where I would be living full time. There would be no weekend visits. Maybe I would get home once before Christmas. I also knew that this was going to be a big sacrifice for my mother to make financially. She always had to count every penny, but had a strong faith in God. This was something she wanted for her daughter believing that God would help her provide for the necessary fees involved. There were no discussions to be had as a firm decision by mother had been made.

Mother was a regular listener to this school's radio broadcasts on Sunday mornings. Through them she had become familiar with the school's offerings and had been impressed. She decided that ninth grade would be the year I was to begin my attendance.

This independent training center was not connected with any church denomination. The founder, a charismatic personality originating from Kansas City, Kansas, was independent in his thinking yet not radical in a negative way. The school had a Baptist format in its organization but was a training center for missionaries. Their graduates served with many independent but well known missionary organizations around the world. Some missions were connected with traditional church denominations, but many graduate students served under independent boards. The graduate students were readily accepted and sought after by these boards because of the training and reputation which the school had.

Why the founder left Kansas going north to the central Alberta prairie land locating next to a small town with few services, was a decision few understood. In all probability it had to do with the availability of land, its price, and the kind of vision he had for this training center.

In order to keep tuition and boarding fees down for students their management system was innovative. A farm was developed enabling them to raise their own beef and grow vegetables, particularly potatoes, for both students and staff. All students were expected to work daily for an hour and a half in some kind of service for the school. Each student was assigned a gratis job for the year. This student requirement was a variation of the norm for keeping costs down.

My first year job was peeling potatoes. It amounted to removing eyes and bits of peel left by the automatic potato peeler. Several students, about fifteen, served this daily routine in a large utilitarian room standing by long tables while several automatic peelers did the tumbling. It took a lot of potatoes to feed eleven hundred students, plus several hundred staff members.

This school also sent undergraduate students from their college department out to local communities where no local churches existed and were unable to afford the service of a full time minister. Usually a center for worship was a former closed down country school, a building no longer in use as a result of reorganization within the provincial education system. A country school house missionary church was my first church experience but our family was not regular attendees. Most of the time any spiritual influence in our family came from listening to a religious radio program on Sunday mornings.

Preparation was made and now completed for departure with all of my personal items packed and ready to load into our pickup truck. My mother drove me the two hours it took to reach this new experience for me at boarding school. This change seemed like a continuation of the life changes which I had already experienced so much of. Sharing a dorm room with a girl whom I had never met was just an information statement in my mind.

When mother left, homesickness did not enter my thinking. There would be no phone calls only an exchange of letters now and then. We did not talk about when we would see each other again knowing that it would be awhile. As it turned out I got home once before Christmas for a weekend.

My first floor dormitory room was sparsely furnished with the basics. A set of bunk beds, two chests of drawers, one for each occupant, closet, desk to be shared with your roommate and a window. I was used to fresh air so having a window to open for air exchange was a feature that I took note of. The fact that my roommate might not need as much fresh air as me never crossed my mind but as we got to know each other the state of the window never became an issue.

Social life would be confined to campus life with no dating allowed for high school students. Contact between the two sexes was strictly forbidden and kept very separate.

Silent Tears

The same evening of arrival my roommate showed up and I learned that she was a junior who was from a prairie region small town located in a central part of the province. Our backgrounds were similar as we both had the rural experience. Our relationship was a neutral one but managed to relate with each other without any friction.

She was studious, spending her time in an efficient manner. I got my homework done but I wasn't the motivated student that she was. I preferred spending my time in the girl's gym or taking long walks down the railway tracks. The girl's gym was new for me and I discovered that I enjoyed the physical exercise while at the same time I was developing a sports ability which I didn't know I had. Before boarding school I had played on the girls softball team, did a lot of ice skating, curling at the curling rink, and horseback riding, but never before had a gym available on a continuous basis.

Living full time on campus offered exposures that blew my limited small town experience wide open. Every year I had a new roommate. One of which was a missionary's daughter whose parents had served in China but left for political reasons. She and her brother had left Asia riding an ocean liner by themselves, arriving in Vancouver then making their way to the school's campus.

This private school offered such a wide variety of experiences and I found real relief from the dysfunctional family life I was so used to. The continual arguing between my parents created such a negative environment I dreaded to be in their presence. Being apart was helping to provide a calmer, more peaceful, and structured surrounding where I could absorb some different thought processes. Life could be viewed from some different perspectives.

This was the first time I had ever been exposed to a multi-racial community. Everyone respected each other no matter what race you were or what country you came from. Our student body president came from London with his heavy English accent. My gym teacher was an

African-American lady from Kansas. A girl with whom I became good friends with was from Japan and another was from Nebraska. I discovered that people the world over are the same, have the same needs, and want the same for themselves. I learned that in God's family there is no room for racism. We are all created by God and our original parents were Adam and Eve, who had the first dysfunctional family. I learned that God has a better plan for each of us if we will open our hearts and minds to His calling. He has a plan that replaces the dysfunctional one.

Chapel speakers were another eye-opener for those of us who were living underexposed lives. One speaker who stands out in my mind had managed to escape the Chicago Mafia while deeply participating in the organized crime scene. After going to a Billy Graham Crusade, he came to the conclusion that his life was headed in the wrong direction. Reviewing his life, he knew he must make a change but leaving the gangster lifestyle could mean execution for him because the mind-set of the mafia members is trapped. He knew he could not continue this criminal lifestyle so decided to leave regardless of the cost. Remarkably, he was able to walk away with no threats from his old pals, a miracle to relish for the rest of his life. To hear the testimony of this changed life through a step of faith in Christ was a story that could challenge anyone in their thinking. His was a story to remember.

Even though chapel and church services were patterned after the Baptist format, I learned later the founder did not necessarily think like a Baptist. On some Sunday mornings in our large fifteen hundred seat auditorium our high school principal preached. That would not seem unusual except that the speaker was a woman. In traditional church denominations women were not allowed to preach but with me being unaware of this controversy I thought this was normal. Normal that is, until my husband and I moved to Wisconsin and ran into some real opinionated male church members who held an extremely conservative view. Women were to be treated like children; seen and not heard. I was totally caught off guard and had to rethink this subject. What I had considered to be normal I found was anything but.

A woman's role in the church was a subject which I had never before considered. These rigid attitudes had caught me off guard. I had accepted women preaching as a normal act, but when learning the apparent errors of my ways from these authoritarian thinkers, it was an affront to my mind. The question I had to ask myself was, "How can sincere people holding the same basic spiritual concepts have such different convictions on the same subject?" I had not witnessed such dogma before. I concluded that I had to do my own study on this subject for my own satisfaction, as I really did not know what to think. Being confronted by male church leaders in a very authoritarian manner for stating an opinion was more than unsettling. After my study, I came to the conclusion there is a big difference between Bible doctrine and church doctrine. In short, I concluded these attitudes were based on church doctrine, man's interpretation of Biblical concepts. I needed to give credit to the school's founder for being Biblically earnest while standing by his own convictions. He was ahead of his time; a real visionary.

Each school year was an enriching experience for me. The classroom courses offered and the exposure to really good music presented by talented students either in chapel or church services helped me gain an appreciation for highly skilled musicians. Student interconnectedness plus the special banquets reserved for the junior and senior classes to be honored, capsulated the positive environment provided by the school. At my junior banquet I got to wear my mended dress which had gone through the devastating tornado, the one I had retrieved from the aspen tree.

High school seniors were required to take a public speaking course. Having to speak before the entire high school three hundred plus student body was a challenge but also a refining experience, helping to round out and polish a person's persona.

Selma J. Stroebel

My time at this private school was ending and graduation was coming. Everyone had plans, sending their invitations for the ceremony and I sent mine. Graduation night came and I was the only one with no family members as guests. My father showed up at four o'clock in the morning to pick me up. At the time their non-attendance did not bother me, but later it bothered me a great deal. Feeling that my time away had been a real sacrifice to our family relationships, I had so wanted them to taste some of the richness I had been privy to. I had been away from home for so many days of my life, that this was something I really wanted to share with them. As time moved on the void grew deeper.

My father dropped me off at my grandparents. My grandfather was all excited that I was now going to be home. He and my grandmother had breakfast ready and waiting plus he informed me that he had a surprise. Sitting by my breakfast plate I noticed a package all wrapped up in brown utility paper tied with twine. I opened the package little by little wondering what could possibly be inside. I could tell that this gift was a Grandpa idea. Unfolding the last flap of paper out plopped a pair of hip waders for fishing. This was more than a hint regarding fishing plans for the two of us. I couldn't help but laugh.

Grandpa had another plan for the day. He wanted me to go coyote hunting with him as he had found an active den. Since I had been up all night, all I wanted to do was sleep. He could see that my enthusiasm wasn't overflowing for his idea but was fading into a dying death as I fell asleep sitting in my chair. His gift and hunting idea was a humorous act, creating a fond memory of a person who was my idol. We did do some fishing together in Big Red after I woke up.

After graduation I felt the need to stay home and help mother. She had sacrificed much for my benefit and was generous with her support for things she believed in. I read in the school paper about a lady who had sent a donation to the school along with a note stating that she would continue to put a fork in her oven door to keep it closed rather than buy a new one. Then I recognized author of that letter as being my mother.

Staying home after graduation was helpful to mother but disastrous for me. My melancholy spirit sent me over the edge emotionally into full fledged depression, a name I now know for that condition. Life was no longer worth living. I was trapped in my own deeply depressed state of mind with no hope for any kind of change in my life. At the end of that year I knew that I needed to go back to school.

Establishing My Own Faith

BEING SURROUNDED by those who spoke of faith, preached faith, left missionary training and went to a mission field by faith, was a concept that was difficult for me to internalize. Living side by side with all of these examples and testimonials didn't make it personal to me. It was not a belief I could stake my life on. Faith seemed to be too abstract of a concept.

There is more to this spiritual life than I understood I concluded. There would not be this many students and staff staking their lives voluntarily on the faith principle. Students believed voluntarily without coercion. They were choosing life paths that would require a lot of self-sacrifice. Choosing to take Christ's sacrificial love story to tribes on islands under very difficult and many times life threatening circumstances and being led by the faith they testified to seemed too extreme for me to accept at the time. Visiting speakers were also sharing amazing stories that were personal and offered challenges.

Cerebrally I believed these teachings were true, observing the positive responses from fellow students and staff. However, I remained a doubting Thomas as there were questions I needed an answer to. Does God truly exist? Is the Bible truly God's letter to us? According to the Biblical teaching, I'm in trouble with God. Is there really a place called Hell? Can I really trust Him for forgiveness and eternal life? What if all of this religious teaching is nothing more than a good story?

The thought did not cross my mind to search for God trying to decide whether He existed or not. Rather I said to myself through a simple prayer, "God if you truly exist then prove to me that you do." Without realizing what I had done in that moment, I had shifted the responsibility of proving God's existence from me to Him. Giving God the job of proving Himself is what He desires, as that is His job.

Letting God prove Himself has been the most amazing life trip that can be imagined. There have been many God whispers throughout my days giving me answers to my questions, answering them beyond my expectations. The whispers of truth gave me more than I had asked in removing my doubting Thomas mindset. An amazing spiritual principle I learned about God is that He is waiting to be asked to be involved in our lives so that He can prove Himself to us personally. Keeping the door closed to Him will only keep Him on the wrong side of the door, never being able to find the life He has planned for us. He is a treasure found beyond compare and beyond our imaginations. Christ said, "I am the Way, the Truth, and the Life".

Life's maturing process teaches us that God's drugstore has amazing healing remedies. One prescription which He issued for me was found in the book of Joshua.

Have not I commanded you to be strong, courageous, do not be terrified, nor discouraged, for the Lord thy God is with you wherever you go? Joshua 1:9

This verse covers every human emotion that one can possibly have. It has been an effective remedy for my own depressive tendencies. I have tried to make it the foundation of every path I have chosen.

Virginia Edna Fletcher-- Nee--Thompson

1905-1999

The Woman I Remember--My Mother

MOTHER AND HER BIG IDEA became apparent one mid-spring day when my parents picked me up after school, informing me that we were headed to Southern Alberta to visit some sheep ranches. Mother stated the plan was to increase the existing number to our current herd by using old ewes as their price would be affordable. My parents apparently discussed this whole idea long before I became aware. Knowing the two of them, this would be mother's big idea while my father would have listened and verbalized a few words of approval, not that mother would have needed it.

We drove all evening and through the long nighttime hours, both taking their turns sharing the driving of our 1947 Willey's jeep. This was a surplus vehicle left over from World War II. We had no money to stay in a hotel so we had to keep traveling.

We finally arrived at a sheep ranch about two hundred and fifty miles from our river land home. I don't remember stopping to eat anywhere as the green stuff was very limited. Whenever we would be on the road traveling mother would have my father stop at a deli where she would buy sliced head cheese. Not a favorite of mine, however, that head cheese managed to keep body and soul together. Regardless of how I disliked the taste, texture, the lack of visual appeal, it was always mother's method of satisfying the appetite.

Silent Tears

Arriving at a sheep ranch, touring with Mother while in a discourse with the owner, my father and I listened following along. This ten year old mind was not taking a whole lot in at this point. This just seemed to be another experience of a different kind providing an expansion and interruption to the daily routine of life on our ranch. Even in our routine the unexpected seemed to happen almost daily.

Only after the tour ended did I begin to internalize the details of what had just happened. After boarding our Jeep my parents began discussing the logistics of how to manage this new adventure.

As the information began to enter my ears, I learned that Mother had just purchased a thousand old ewes from this rancher and was having them shipped by rail to the nearest railroad town. The closest railroad station happened to be twenty five miles from our pasture land. This herd of one thousand sheep would have to be driven the remaining distance. How was mother going to accomplish this grand undertaking, I was wondering to myself? Her solution to this problem was to hire some native Canadian Indians to aid in driving these wooly creatures from the railway yard to our recently acquired three hundred and twenty acre plot of land we named, "The Eagle Valley Property." After arriving at the pasture land with all of these woolly critters, these natives were to become sheepherders, protecting them from the many coyotes that loved to hide in the lowland brush.

The first problem which had to be dealt with was the railroad stockyard. The station didn't have enough stock pens to accommodate one thousand sheep. Everyone involved would have to be available upon the sheep's arrival, keeping them under control while trying to maneuver the wooly crowd through and out of town. Driving them down the road worked as long as you could physically lead one with the rest usually following. Not living at home during this part of the family adventure, I never heard how they provided food and water for this three day sheep drive. I did hear about the sheep being afraid of bushes on the pasture land since they had lived on the prairie where no bushes existed. In time they did adjust.

In time, the goal of Mother's method became an understandable concept learning that her plan was to breed these ewes for a one year lamb and wool crop. After weaning and shearing time, these old ewes would then all be marketed when they were ready. She figured this strategy would be an economical method of increasing the family herd. After the lamb crop arrived, and weaning and culling completed, she would have young stock without laying out the cost for such. The timing of this cycle would be important in providing an income from the sheared fleece before the old ewes were shipped.

The Eagle Valley Ranch land possessed a lot of topographical variety with fields of tillable land, some steep hills, a picturesque flat land meadow, bogs that were formed by a beaver dammed creek, and another creek that provided a good supply of fresh water. These beaver dams formed marshes that were continually wet making it impossible to cross through these areas except when frozen during winter months. No animal could wade through this marsh as they would sink into the mud up to their bellies, getting stuck. However, for me, this piece of property with its many characteristics was a natural draw for exploring by horseback.

When this land came up for sale my mother jumped at the opportunity to purchase it. How she did it I don't know as I never heard her explain. I knew her father believed you could never go wrong purchasing land. In his mind land was always a good investment. In all probability it was due to his advice. I do know that the land could not have cost much; however, my gut tells me the purpose of this purchase was the same as her big idea of expanding her herd of sheep. She wanted and needed more land for her business ideas.

This property was the first home for these one thousand prairie raised sheep staying there for the next year. Through the rest of the summer the native Canadians continued with their sheepherding. When fall came my parents made the decision to spend the winter on this property, living in the bachelor's cabin. A major motive for this decision was the small barns and corrals providing facilities needed for lambing time along with a supply of winter feed which my father had harvested from those tillable fields.

How they managed to live in this one room cabin is a tale of living on the earthy side of life. They had no running water, no indoor plumbing, no kitchen counter, only a make shift cabinet, a free standing wood stove, along with two bunk beds padded with straw as a mattress. A few household items were moved from the River Land to help make the stay possible. Needless to say, I didn't miss home.

That winter spent under these rustic conditions was a tremendous challenge for mother. I do not know if she envisioned the mammoth amount of work involved or not. Lambing time in the middle of the winter for a thousand plus population of ewes is a job for a team of people. For a team of two with that much responsibility is a job for the mind that has become delusional. Mother spent many all night sessions in those barns with temps dipping well below zero. It was very important for newborns to be on their feet and nursing soon after birth. My father was a helper but not the all-nighter mother was.

Orphan lambs were always part of the scene for one reason or another requiring special care since the mother did not survive the birth process. Humans have to become the substitute parent with a big bottle filled with cow's milk and a large nipple on the end. This job alone can keep a person busy for a significant portion of your day.

Lambing time is not the only event on the calendar that keeps life on a sheep ranch busy. Diseases require vaccinations. Then comes tick control. Ticks love the warm lanolin environment provided by the wool where they can feed undetected on the host's body. Left untreated the ticks cause skin irritation. When an infestation exists each wooly critter has to be dipped in a vat of tick treatment. With such a large herd, a lot of vat dipping went on for a number of days.

Just about the time you think you can take a breather from sheep duty there is another event that appears on the calendar. Long wool starts to grab your attention, staring you in the face giving you a call for another duty to be taken care of. Long wool in hot summer temps becomes very uncomfortable for the animal so a spring shearing schedule becomes apparent and the animal care calendar continues to roll.

Shearing involves personally handling each animal to hand clip off the past year's layer of wool growth. This was one of those times when my parents would hire outside help. Native Canadians were accustomed to that kind of work, so employing them for the shearing season made sense. The women worked beside the men performing this task. There was no sex discrimination for this kind of employment.

During shearing days, Mother would become chief cook and bottle washer. The custom was the shearer's wages included the dinner meal. My thought would be bring your own bag lunch as I'm not cooking. Mother would think that attitude would not be a hospitable one. She always wanted to be considerate of everyone regardless of whether it was a business occasion or a social event.

The lady shearer let it be known that only a certain kind of canned stew was acceptable. She was insistent and mother obliged. Mother purchased one can of stew with the correct brand name label leaving it visible for all the prepared meals. Analyzing the ingredients, mother reproduced the commercial stew. The flavor must have been the same only now with an affordable price and the female shearer never knew the difference.

With the shearing project completed, marketing the wool came next. Each wool bat, one from each sheep, had to be rolled and tied with twine readying it for being placed in a very large burlap sack. Each burlap sack held about ten newly shorn fleece which were then loaded onto my father's pickup truck for the many trips to the shipping center. This would also be the time that my grandmother received wool fleece for all of her quilt making.

Hired help was a limited service for our family. Shearing and herding were the only times where a feeling of respite could be enjoyed. Even though help was always hired for shearing there were times when we provided our own herding. When coyotes are a problem, defenseless sheep cannot be left alone. When I was home in the summer, herding duty became one of my chores.

A job description for this occupation is described with one word -BORING. You can only do so much talking to your dog before the dog doesn't want to listen anymore. There are only so many molehills to kick with you boot or stones to throw at the field gophers. Even the clouds in the sky hold your imagination for just so long. Imagining different images of the clouds only to watch them reshape themselves into a different form can hold your interest for a brief time. Music wasn't available. Our only radio was run by a very large battery back at the house and listening time was rationed as that battery had to last a year.

Centuries ago sheep herders found this job to be as exciting as I did. They learned to pass their time by using sticks to move and toss stones back and forth to each other. Thus, this was the beginning and the birth of our modern day sport of golf.

Mother, as a Business Woman:

When Mother made the decision to purchase that large number of old ewes from a southern Alberta ranch, it was a decision made after a lot of research and planning.

Mother was one of those people who had a pencil, eraser, and a pad of paper in her hand almost constantly for a definite purpose. Her mind was always churning on how she could make a dollar. I can see her in my memory, sitting on the kitchen stool with a pencil and a pad of paper on her lap. Meal planning and housework took second place during her day. When an idea would come to her mind she would write it down, do the math, figure possible profits and losses, and always calculate her risks.

Selma J. Stroebel

Mother subscribed to farm publications to keep in touch with markets and production conditions all across Canada and the United States. She studied current markets of supply and demand as well as the predictions for the future. She studied whatever was failing and sought ways to capitalize on that. Whatever was an oversupplied product, forcing the price in a downward trend was the product she planned to start producing. She said that by the time she got her production going, others would be going out of production, resulting in price increases. There would be her profit.

She had a willingness to experiment by trying new things and obviously didn't shrink from the work that it entailed. She had the capacity to think out of the box, doing what was unheard of for a woman of her time. She built up credit with her bank. This enabled her to go to the bank and borrow any amount of money that she applied for. She always made sure that she repaid her debt before it was due. As a result, whenever she applied for a loan the officer would ask her, "How much do you need?" They didn't set the limit on her borrowing; she set her own limits. Through her tenacity and hard work she proved herself to be a very responsible person, something that bankers and loan officers like.

She kept meticulous records in case she was audited by the tax department, which happened several times due to the kind of return she submitted. Self-employed returns are subject to the lottery system of being selected more often for an audit. However, after auditing her books, she was left alone again for a time.

Her extensive knowledge in the veterinary field came about through her own personal interest in medicine. Since the human side of medicine was a closed field for her, the field of veterinary medicine was an alternative. Ordering books through the mail to study on her own related to the different species she was working with as well as her close association with the local vet clinic, provided the much needed source of information she sought. This was basically her training ground for her extensive knowledge. I have always regretted for my mother that she was unable to pursue her primary medical interest. I know that she would have been a great medical doctor. She definitely had the mindset and will for that professional field of service.

I have seen my mother milling through the animal pens watching for anything that was amiss. I can hear her say, "Something is wrong with----." She would be right every time. She would proceed with her own personally devised solution for treatment by going to her own inventory of medications stored on a shelf in our back hall of the old farm house. Living an inconvenient distance away from the veterinary clinic, she worked to keep her own supply on hand with shelves covered with all kinds of medicines for many different kinds of problems, along with any paraphernalia that would be needed for administering the drugs. Her private pharmacy was a store house for the miscellaneous. I'll say it this way, our back hall was not a scene from Better Homes and Gardens.

This extensive knowledge which she had built up gave her the foundation she needed for her other adventures besides the sheep herd idea. She would raise large flocks of turkeys to meet the Thanksgiving market, and chickens for the egg market. To take advantage of a larger and different poultry market, she studied how to turn a rooster into a capon. They would command a higher price at the meat counter.

With the sheep business now established, Mother was continuing to manage the medical needs in order to keep the animals healthy. Another aspect of her study of was in the area of animal nutrition. Good or poor nutrition affected the animal's health which in turn affected profit margins. Also, an awareness of the special nutritional needs had to be a priority for a healthy reproduction of the young, again affecting profit margins.

My father continued with his chores, riding his pinto pony to move sheep from one grazing field to another, or driving them to water a couple times a day. Sometimes he would forget and leave a gate open or neglect to repair a hole in a fence, allowing the sheep to wander into the wrong field. Normally, it is not a big deal unless the very adverse alfalfa legume is involved, affecting ruminants (cud chewing animals), with sudden bloating and death. More than once that happened with substantial losses. My father had a way of keeping us all on edge by causing some kind of an emergency because of something he either did or didn't do. We were continually exasperated. We interpreted these occasions as being careless. However, he did manage to deal with daily routine with some measure of success where an emergency did not result.

The original old ewes were now marketed. Younger ones now populated the herd. Mother's strategy had worked and her goal met. However, Mother never liked to be locked into one idea. Even though she had reached her original goal, a new idea emerged to improve both wool and meat production. She introduced a breed of ram that was known for its wool growth and another stockier one for better mutton production. To introduce those characteristics, a number of ewes were chosen by dividing and selecting at breeding time.

The sheep business was a part of their lives until my father passed away at the age of eighty-three. Only a few sheep remained on the farm at that time and that was for old time's sake.

Overlapping the sheep business were some of mother's other endeavors as an outgrowth of her market research and studies. This was all a part of her, "Plan Ahead Strategy." One year she raised five hundred turkeys to meet the autumn Thanksgiving markets. Hundreds of chickens were also an endeavor one year and, never to be eliminated were the duck raising efforts.

Amazing insights into animal personalities are discovered when one is deeply involved with their daily care, and when they are allowed to live a free-range life. Turkeys love to go for walks with you. All you have to do is go where they are and start walking down a lane. Several times I took mother's five hundred turkeys for a walk out into the grassy field. That is one way to eliminate any kind of insect infestation, especially grasshoppers.

Silent Tears

Mother's other adventurer---The Auction Mart

I do not know where the idea for her next adventure came from. One day Mother explained that we were going to an auction mart located in Calgary near the stockyards. Being about eleven years old at the time, the three of us climbed into our Willy's jeep and headed out. I learned there was an auction taking place every Saturday.

Bovine babies, which were extras from nearby dairy farms, were being auctioned. Mature stock was also being sold but mother's focus was always the newborn or the very young.

Mother would walk through the aisles of small pens, studying the contents. Men would be doing the same but having their discussions with each other. Mother would eavesdrop on their conversations in a non-obtrusive manner, learning about the dairy business and the importance of a calf's conformation, as well as other information good to know. By using her bent ear, Mother claimed she learned a lot from these men, honing her skill of knowing how to learn.

By the end of the day, I could count on the fact that mother would buy herself a calf, and the words, "Sold to Mrs. Fletcher," would echo from the auctioneer's lips. We became regular attendants.

This newly purchased calf would ride home with us in the back of our Willy's Jeep, wrapped up in a burlap bag for safe travel. Arriving home, Mother would immediately place this new bovine resident in isolation. Invariably, these youngsters would pick up an easily transmitted disease from those never disinfected auction mart pens. With mother's knowledge and experience, she was not fazed a bit. She just went to her personal pharmacy, pulling the meds off the shelf, and proceeded to treat her patient. Within a couple of weeks the isolation period would end.

Many Saturdays my parents and I headed to Calgary taking in these auctions and invariably Mother would come home with a new purchase. Having done her eavesdropping and learning a lot about picking out a good producing milk cow while still a baby, became an art by refining her thinking. After awhile, she became very astute.

These trips to the mart became our source to grow a cattle herd; however, her plan for the herd involved a different concept, a non-traditional idea. My father had accumulated some beef stock while working for his father, but monetarily was not profitable even though they numbered about one hundred. The goal was to reduce that number, thus was the birth of mother's idea.

Her plan was to let these calves grow until they reached the age of two years. Then the males would be shipped to market and the heifers sold privately. Advertising these soon-to-deliver-a -baby young cows could command a good price, and they did. Milk producers liked being able to pick up young, ready-to-produce milkers. Her marketing strategy was just an ad in the newspaper. No longer did my parents plan to maintain a long-term herd of aging stock. This plan was much more profitable.

Auction mart days also provided some unexpected benefits. Being able to go down-town Calgary to the open air street markets after the auctions proved to be profitable. Closing time was five o'clock on Saturday night, not opening again until Monday morning. Mother would take advantage of their closing time deals. Fruit that is close to being overripe, will not keep for two days. Mother was able to take advantage of all kinds of deals as a result. When the price was still too high she pretended to walk away. Within seconds the street dealer would call her back, offering a better price.

Going home with cases of pears and peaches, along with twenty four pounds of bananas for a dollar was like walking out of a candy store. Our garden had been destroyed so many times by the hailstorms, that having this source of fruit was like manna from heaven. Mother would stay up all night canning after her long day at the markets. These fruits had ripened to a point that delaying preservation would render them unfit for canning. By the time winter came, she would have canned more than four hundred quart jars of various fruits becoming a staple through the winter. This practice continued for several years.

During this time Mother continued to practice her knowledge of veterinary medicine, animal nutrition, and her business skills. Success came her way often, but it was also often that huge obstacles would present themselves due to my father's condition; a condition that no one understood. Determination and the spirit of forging ahead was what she was always about.

Mother was so used to living a frugal lifestyle that she expected the same of others. During one of our summer visits I stated I wanted to replace her dull paring knife. While struggling to peel some potatoes, that comment sent her into a state of perplexity. Her reply to my statement was, "All you want to do is spend money." I said nothing, knowing how hard she had worked all of her life just to survive. She related to me another time how she had deposited one dollar at a time into her savings account. I have also heard her say, "Thank You Lord that I have enough money to pay my bills." Her spiritual focus was always a preeminent characteristic of the life she lived.

Mother and her health problems:

Mother spent much of her time outdoors, doing what men normally do. Working very hard physically would give the impression that she was a strong robust woman with lots of muscle strength and a strong constitution; someone who wore denim overalls and leather work boots. One could also visualize her with long, grey, braided hair, rolled up in a bun for easy styling and convenience. You could expect mannerisms to match and speech that could be on the coarse side. However, in reality mother was totally the opposite. She loved style, good taste, and possessed an educated vocabulary. A petite woman, always dressed as a lady in a dress and dress coat, even when she went to the auction mart. Her hair was a golden auburn with natural bends, kept short, and always styled. Being lady-like was very important to her. She would quietly criticize those women who let themselves become coarse. This was her way of saying they were trying to act like men rather than retaining their femininity.

Mother loved being outdoors claiming she could breathe easier. When indoors, it was a constant struggle to get enough oxygen. The lack of oxygen causing her shortness of breath, were statements she often repeated. Chest pains and an irregular heartbeat were some other complaints continuously verbalized. These same symptoms were apparent during her high school years while doing advanced studies in order to prepare herself for entering medical school. Difficulty in breathing, chest pains, and fatigue seemed to remain a life-long condition but also disqualified her entry into the one and only desired field of education.

The medical field lacked research results pertaining to cardiac conditions. She did not seek medical help after her medical school physical rejection. With the opening of a local health food store, she became a frequent customer, treating herself with herbal remedies. This self-treatment helped to relieve some of her symptoms but they never completely vanished. Always keeping a stash of brandy and herbs to ease her cardiac problems was her mainstay for self treatment, making it somewhat possible to manage and control the severity of her symptoms.

A swig of brandy helped to relieve her chest pain symptoms. Brandy was used only for this medicinal purpose she was quick to state. Being a teetotaler by religious conviction, made it embarrassing for her to shop for her supply, always shopping in a town where she was not known. Afraid that her supply would dwindle too low, an effort was made to purchase a bottle whether she needed it or not when away from her local community. When she passed away at the age of ninety three, we found ten bottles of brandy camouflaged and stored at the back of her closet enveloped in my father's old socks. She considered her supply to be her secret, not wanting anyone to know that her stash was that well-supplied. If anyone opened the closet door none would be visible.

Silent Tears

With current medical knowledge, her cardiac problems could have been diagnosed and treated. Perhaps she would even have been able to pursue the medical career she had dreamed of, that of being a medical missionary doctor. Not being able to pursue her first love of medicine was a huge disappointment. She had referred to this disappointment many times.

Looking back into her life, I am disappointed for her. I comprehend more clearly her talents, intelligence, persistence, and personal discipline. She would have been very capable of being the medical doctor she dreamed of.

I am awed by how hard mother worked to provide for her family under the obstacles she faced. There were so many ways she deprived herself in order for me to have an education and a life that could be better than hers. Living with other families was a weekly bill for her to meet and residing in the private school was even a much larger bill to undertake. She knew something was wrong with my father's ability for having a successful business and in helping to manage the agrarian lifestyle. Regardless, she plowed forward with determination in spite of the many obstacles that many times presented themselves as an impossible mountain to climb.

An example of an impossible mountain to climb comes to mind with the occasion of treating a steer that had contracted black leg; a fatal bovine disease that destroys the muscle of the leg and can be identified by a crinkling texture under the skin. Cattlemen know how important the control of this disease is through vaccinations, or a herd can be devastated. Mother was told by the veterinarians that treatment was futile. Mother followed her gut by first isolating the animal, and then proceeded with her personal treatment plan until recovery was attained. Her efforts had paid off proving she could never be called a quitter.

I also appreciate the spiritual legacy which she left as an example for her family to follow. Her deep faith was expressed daily through her lifestyle. She spoke often of truths learned from reading her Bible and miracle stories of faith she either read about or heard though friends. She readily spoke of her own miracle of healing from the pain of shingles and rheumatoid arthritis; the autoimmune disease that persisted in crippling her body. Also, she never neglected to share that you were included in her daily prayers. Her faith was the foundation on which she built her life.

Even though a strong faith can be a part of our lives, forks in the road of life present themselves, forcing us to make decisions. Down the road of life we can self-doubt ourselves in regards to those decisions made during those important times of our lives. This was the case with my mother in marrying my father when reviewing in her mind how the realities of her life were very different than what she had ever envisioned.

Because of the extensive daily dysfunction on our farm, unfortunately it took me a very long time to grow into a real appreciation of the gifts my mother possessed. How she was able to deal with the daily stresses awes me continuously.

My father's inability to independently function beyond the daily routine of everyday life was beyond my capacity to understand. I had a lot of whys in my mind with no answers. However, I never gave up watching for clues that could possibly provide some insights.

Because mother never received the normal emotional support from her spouse that is a part of any marriage relationship, she began to depend on me for her sounding board. When her frustrations built up to the blowing point with the need to unload, I became her dumping ground claiming that I was the only one she had. Her many disappointments and baffling situations, all would continue to mount until she unloaded those pent-up emotions that could no longer be contained. When she began to dump, there would be a lot to internalize. Encompassing everything from my father's irresponsibility, his lack of caring for the family and his seeming appearance to pretend to others that he cared when she believed he didn't. His spending and losing money which we didn't have and her being blamed for driving him crazy by his family added to the emotional mountain. Our local community did not care or understood our situation, either. Her mammoth dump would leave a black cloud hanging over my head.

Listening to her frustrations began to have a real negative effect on me emotionally. Recalling an evening when I was about ten years old, one such event took place as my mother was severely down in the dumps. Being that it was dusk, with the coal oil lamp still unlit, I was able to sit on the old boot box and listen in the growing darkness. I was glad that it was becoming darker with daylight quickly fading. I was determined to not let her know that I was shedding silent tears for her. I felt so bad that she was so unhappy and was being accused of driving my father crazy, made my feelings much more intense and drove my hurt deeper for her. Inside, I knew that it was totally untrue. She deserved so much more respect than she was receiving. All I had to offer during those moments were my listening ears and my silent tears.

This hard working woman had done so much. This woman who was so intelligent, but feeling like she was wasting her life. Questioning and self doubting as to how she could have been so stupid as to have married my father. So, as I sat and listened on many occasions, all I could do was shed my silent tears in sorrow for her.

I am now aware that these difficult and burdensome moments in my life as a child were the times when seeds were being planted and giving root to my own struggle with depression. The groundwork of hopelessness was being laid and my own my emotional spiral downward had begun. My mother's unhappiness became my focus for many years to come, causing me to neglect my emotional growth and well-being. Recalling these scenes in my mind, I clearly see that I was a child pulled into adult-sized problems without the coping skills needed to deal with the complexity of these circumstances; nor was there anyone around me to form a shield of protection that could have been a buffer with some understanding of life with its realism. Instead my silent tears flowed copiously for my mother.

Mother's heart problems had decidedly affected her life. Her stressful lifestyle was another negative factor affecting, without question, her psychological health. Totaling these factors together, there is currently evidence that autoimmune diseases can be triggered by prolonged stressful circumstances. Rheumatoid arthritis became her constant companion, a resident in her life that would not leave. In her mid- fifties this new companion took up residence, causing a lot of pain and producing deformities throughout her whole body. Her hands, hips, back, knees, feet, and eventually even her eyes were affected. She did receive some relief from new medications being introduced.

Like every other obstacle that mother faced, she fought back. At the end of her life, she made the following statement to me, "Life has been on the hard side." My thought, which went unexpressed was, "In your case, I think so."

I am convinced that mother's early life health problems, plus the unsettled family dynamics during her own growing up years being shrouded in turmoil, affected her decision making process. Her clouded judgment when dating my father and his disguised symptoms became a recipe for an unrecognizable reality. After much questioning in my mind, these are some conclusions I have come to.

Frances Arthur Dennis Fletcher

June 19, 1904--April 23, 1987
My Father

The Man I Remember

THE OLD-FASHONED wall phone in my parent's sitting room was ringing. It awakens me. I'm groggy from traveling after spending nearly three days on the road. Our family had arrived late the previous evening from Wisconsin. It keeps ringing. "Should I answer?" I ask myself. I see that it is eight o'clock in the morning and the Alberta sun is already high in the sky. It is mid-summer in Alberta and daylight comes very early, starting shortly after four a.m. The phone rings again. "Where is mother?" I think in my mind. The phone keeps ringing. I assess that she is outside doing her morning chores. I decide to crawl out of bed and answer the phone.

"Hello," there is a halting response on the other end of the line. Again, I say, " Hello." "I want to speak to Edna." I now recognize the voice as that of my father. My response is, "Hello dad, this is Selma." He again responds with, "I want to speak to Edna." I try again by saying "Hello dad, this is your daughter, Selma." I get the same response, "I want to speak to Edna." I now comprehend that he is not recognizing my voice. Now my reply is, "Hold on, I will get her," as I'm confirming that I would do what he asked.

As I go searching for my mother, it is quickly running through my mind we have a serious problem. I had never before experienced him not recognizing my voice. Have things disintegrated this much, or has mother been hiding what she does not want us to know? She is good at that.

She responds to my call from one of the chicken coops. As I stand in the yard, I explain that dad is waiting on the phone wanting to talk to her. Refocusing herself to my request, she hurries toward the house. As she runs through the sitting room, her body language tells me that she is upset and saying to herself, "not this again." I'm interpreting this to say, there have been other similar episodes which we have not heard about.

Now my mind spins the thought, "How has she dealt with these episodes when alone and by herself?" I knew that her fear of others knowing would be a reality in her mind, so decided not to ask. Mother, in her independence, always had a way of figuring things out. Her strong will displayed itself through I have my solutions, don't interfere.

Ending her short conversation with my father, she turned toward me stating, "We have to go and get your father." Jim has now risen becoming aware of mother's statement. Jim quickly volunteers to drive mother in our station wagon to wherever. Mother did not state to us where he had gone. Fortunately, we had arrived from Wisconsin late the previous night, making our help available. However, we still did not know what this help entailed. A spirit of somberness filled the room.

This sudden morning wake-up of a different kind, filled the air with uncertainty. Our pre-teens were now alerted to this unusual circumstance of the morning's commotion. They had been excited about our Alberta visit with their grandparents, but in this moment they didn't know what to think and neither did I.

The unusual circumstances of the morning caused me to think about precautions. I clearly was not prepared to think in terms of my father not recognizing me or my voice. What caused this lack of recognition? Was there a threat we needed to consider? This upsetting situation moved me to consider the worst. Do we need to take some security steps? I turned to the kids explaining the circumstances and made the declaration that we were going to hide all the kitchen knives and any guns in the house.

Four hours later my parent's old red Ford truck drove into the driveway with mother behind the wheel. Jim was following her in our station wagon. We were relieved to see them but still very much on edge. A lot of uncertainty hung in the air. There would be no relaxation until the knowing gap was filled.

Silence filled the air. No one knew how to respond or what to say. Speechlessness filled the room. Everyone tried to refocus by proceeding with some normal activity like washing their hands, eating a snack, straightening up the house, or Jim organizing an outdoor project with the children. Everyone was feeling the need to find a way to be comfortable, to normalize. Finally, Jim remarked to me that my father had driven the pickup to a town about seventy five miles away where he had managed to call from a gas station.

"What hour of the morning did he leave the house," I asked myself. Seventy five miles with dad driving is a long way. My father being the slowest driver on the road, hardly ever driving the minimum limit. If he called the house at eight o'clock this morning, he had to have left home no later than five a.m. Did he not sleep all night? How did he know how to make that call? What triggered this episode?

During this somber time, with everyone trying to get back to a normal mental state, my father stepped close to me and made a remark that gave an explanation for his actions. His statement was, "Were they ever after me, and boy did I get away." I did not react, but just listened. My thought was "Where did that threat in your mind come from?" Hallucinations were something I did not understand.

The question remained, confronting us all. What do we do to change his frame of mind, to bring him out of this state of hallucination into normal reality? Without making this question a big issue, everyone involved felt the strong need to be normal themselves, involving him with their normalcy.

Within a couple of hours everyone was beginning to breathe easier. We began to recognize more normal comments coming from my father. He was slowly coming out of his illusionary condition.

My mind was reviewing lesser episodes from the past. Living with the memory of these maladies, recalls your burned out ability of dealing with life, and the depressive thinking which I had lived with so long. The state of my own mind comes back to my memory, even though time had helped me experience a lot of recovery. I was recalling my own mental state but presently no longer did I have to live it. Through many God whispers, God had shown me a path out of my condition but many questions remained. However, mother was still living with it, everyday. My silent tears for her would still flow.

These characteristics which my father would display from time to time were eerie in nature to me. Between irrational behavior episodes, my father could function quite normally. Plowing his fields and doing his cultivating, growing his great stands of grain, and receiving compliments from other farmers for his impressive fields. Routine was his friend most of the time. "Why would he have these swings in behavior," I would ask myself. The movie, "Three Faces of Eve," would come to my mind. I really did not want to believe that my father was similar to the character in the movie. I would continue to watch for clues. I needed some answers. There had to be some somewhere. His problems were affecting and had already affected my own validation.

Happening much earlier in their marriage and sharing with me long after the event, mother related a story concerning my father's behavior lacking any logic.

Mother's laying hens were completely out of feed grain. My father stated he would go first thing in the morning to the feed mill and be back home by nine o'clock in time for feeding. Taking my father at his word seemed to be a viable solution.

Leaving early next morning as planned, my father did not return home by nine as promised, nor at noon, or by evening. At eleven o'clock that night he returned without any chicken feed, with no money, and no explanation. Mother was devastated. Without grain the chickens would stop laying and there would go their grocery money.

These kinds of episodes showing a lack of judgment, or times of disorientation (as in the case of not being able to find the hundred head of hogs being kept in the edge of the pine forest), and lack of focus, seemed to have no real explanations.

Eventually, that swine herd was lost due to my father's carelessness. My father had ordered a load of grain to be delivered by a trucker who had hauled a load of diseased pigs to market. Mother begged my father to cancel this delivery. He refused. She had become aware of this disease through listening in on the community telephone system. Within weeks the herd had to be shipped due to this disease, ending their swine business. Cause and effect relationships seemed to be a concept my father, at times, was unable to grasp.

Three fires three days in a row were started by my father during hot, dry weather conditions that should have told him not to. He started them anyway. The first fire spread to the edge of a bog that created a boundary for spreading flames. On the other side mother and I carried buckets of water enabling us to wet terry towels for slapping spreading flames in the dry grass. Fires double in size within seconds but we managed to get it under control, leaving us totally exhausted. Day two turned out to be a repeat of another out of control fire, but in a different location. Using the same wet towel and water technique mother and I managed to get it under control. Again, mother and I were totally exhausted.

By the end of the second day we assumed my father had realized that burning of old grass and grain stubble was not a safe idea in hot, dry conditions, but best left for a different kind of day. Mother was also letting her opinion be loudly known.

Venting her opinions in an argument with my father did not seem to make much difference. Day three arrived and my father was out there again with his matches starting another fire. Fires do not respect boundaries. Woodland burns just as easily as grass when arid conditions exist. Again mother and I found ourselves fighting to save the woodland using our wet towels and water bucket method. Mother and I were not only concerned with damage to our property but also the danger of these fires spreading to the neighbors. No fire department existed so we were on our own.

My father gave the impression that he had no clue what our problem was. He seemed to completely not understand the dangerous conditions he had created. His one track mind was focused on removing what he did not want to see.

Spring planting season and harvest time were routines that my father could handle without losing his focus. These were routine chores with predictable sun up and sun down time schedules. He loved working the soil, planting his seeds, swathing and binding the standing grain growth, which was a job I was privileged to help him with. Stooking the sheaves of grain gave him a sense of worth and fulfillment to his day. These fixed routine days formed the framework of his life. Being able to function reasonably well within the framework of routine and willing to extend the physical effort to accomplish the tasks before him he never shirked hard physical labor, a great contributing factor for keeping the farm functioning. Severe headaches would sometimes interfere with his farm work commitments. They seemed to be an intermittent, debilitating companion with no seeming explanation for their appearance.

Near normal behavior could last for extended periods of time, diminishing the impact of episodic behavior. During these times, his ability to accomplish routine chores provided a sense of stability for the family. Mother would do the planning; my father would do the listening in a very passive manner. Both mother and I interpreted his non motivated persona as not caring. His contributions to any idea were very limited. Most of the time his response was one of falling asleep. Bringing any idea to pass was accomplished by mother's business mind and her determination to bring them to fruition.

Even though these seemingly normal times would last for extended periods of time, in reality, they were not normal. We as a family had become conditioned. The sub-normal had become normal to us. He would continue to overlook important details. Doors to grain bins would be left open and gates to alfalfa fields would not be closed; resulting in sick animals. Mother would continuously worry about his safety, and when I was at home my job was to check on dad. Farms were havens for severe accidents, so mother would be paranoid for his safety. After he had pinned himself under the tractor wheel in that cold spring water, she became even more vigilant. Building those fires under the tractor in the winter to get it started, would cause mother to feel certain that thing would blow up. After all tractors runs on gas, and the tank usually contained a lot of that explosive mixture. Normal included a crisis of some sort every day. Emotionally, both my mother and I were paying a heavy price. My brother spent a lot of time with our uncle, as well as our grandparents, but left home permanently when he was eighteen.

Mother had the mistaken belief if she talked enough, pointing out shortcomings to my father, he would eventually change. In her mind, self determination could solve almost every problem. It never occurred to her that change would never come. She always believed change was possible, and that one day he would see the light. She was living in self-denial. I never had the courage to tell her that.

Toward the end of her life, while we were having a discussion, I asked a question, "After all that has happened, didn't it ever occur to you that he would never change?" Her response, "How could I have been so stupid?" I had nothing more to say. I knew in her mind that marriage was forever, divorce was out. However, within the context of our discussion, her referral to being stupid had to do with marrying the wrong man. She was now a widow and had a picture of a former boyfriend on her piano. Again, I had sorrowful feelings for her. She was a very talented woman with a deep faith who deserved so much more than what she had experienced.

Yet destiny had taken her down a different path. Was her choice at the fork in the road of her life a mistake or was there a mission before her she failed to see? We could answer for her and say it was definitely a mistake, a wrong choice she made at the time. I prefer to think that simplistic answers sometimes are not answers at all, but only add to the hurt and confusion. Is there still a question that remains unanswered? Could there be some principle to living life that remains uncovered and waiting to be understood? Without my mother's talents, what kind of life would my father have known? I am not going to pretend that I know. I do know that generally he was a happy person, enjoying a life style appropriate for him, living with a contented mind, and oblivious to the problems which surrounded him. Without my mother, in all probability that would not have happened.

Driving my father crazy was a reputation my mother did not deserve. That was something she definitely was not guilty of. However, it was believable. My father's periodic illogical behavior made that rumor acceptable in the eyes of those who knew him. Rural communities and small towns don't have large populations so living one's life anonymously is impossible. Rumors spread like a wildfire, and truth becomes whatever someone says it is. In that case, your life's reputation comes from a created rumor. It is even more believable when it is started by family members, which in this case was my father's family.

It was not until many years later, and after his passing, that some answers would be discovered shedding some light on my father's condition. No official medical diagnosis was ever made during his lifetime. I greatly regret that now. Understanding by those around him could have been so different. Clues and symptoms which I have been able to piece together along with some medical opinions have provided an understandable picture. All came too late for his life to benefit. However, this discovered knowledge gave badly needed explanations for myself and closely related kin.

Medical treatment was only sought one time that I am aware of. My father had been suffering from severe headaches, on and off for years. An x-ray was performed revealing an adhesion on the brain with nothing more determined, no directives, and no follow ups. A dearth of research in the area of psychology existed, however, in time that greatly changed.

Only after many years of my own recovery from depression was I able to be objective regarding my parent's situation. Before my recovery, going back in my mind to review any aspect of the past would literally cause me to become ill for a number of days. I was not able to let my mind go there.

Finding some answers helped me to recover some respect for him. Until then, I had viewed him as being mentally slow, maybe even retarded, and greatly lacking in bringing honor to our family. I felt like I was helping to parent my parent. His unexplainable illogical behavior was embarrassing, all causing me to second guess my own value, a long personal struggle.

Selma J. Stroebel

My father was not any angry man, only very passive. He was not one to fight for himself or his family. He would never verbalize ideas, enjoyed listening to conversations, make a non-original comment, and only occasionally laugh. If you asked him a question, his reply would contain a few words without a meaningful statement. As a result, never in my life did I have a conversation with my father. I had interpreted his ways as not caring or being interested in his family. Our well-being did not seem to be his concern. This became the basis of a lot of anger within myself, and affected my brother as well, adding more stress to my mother's life. Raising an angry boy with little help and understanding from the father did not go well for either my brother or my mother. Their relationship became very strained and caustic.

Our summer visits kept our family connections intact. Our children were able to have a healthy relationship with their grandparents and build some positive memories of them. My parents greatly benefited from time spent with their grandchildren. I was grateful to observe the positive influence working both ways. Through these visits, time spent with them, and the influence of her grandmother, our daughter entered the medical field as a profession.

The following is an essay our daughter wrote for a school assignment. It is her reflection on time spent one evening with her grandfather.

Grandpa:

The crisp cold of the night air fell on the earth with the setting of the sun. The evening sky was wide, stretching over our tiny world. The glorious reds and oranges of the fading sun cast a whole presence on the little farm, a presence of rest and serene quiet, as if to paint its own background for the animals preparing for their rest. Even the trees were still. A most gentle quiet as if heaven were invading the earth, hushing her from her fury.

The shed was cradled on the slope of the hill, as if it always belonged there. And for me it had. A shed that kittens played on, calves rested in, a shed unlike all others. It was a certain kind of home for all who entered its doors. A place that seemed to say, "Come sit for a moment on my manger bed. Come rest, your unquiet thoughts. Step away from all that makes you worry." In here there is a sense of raw importance of life itself. Unpretentious and unaware that most other buildings looked better than it. And frankly, not caring. Yet seemingly totally committed to the life it sheltered from the night's chill.

At night the kittens played in the manger. A cow stood there too, quietly munching on her tuft of hay.

The single light, a lone bulb hanging from the ceiling, casted all the right shadows. The stage was set perfectly. This is where we came. My grandfather and I, to milk the cow.....and talk. He sat on an old tin bucket and methodically milked the cow with an even squirt, squirt, squirt. The plastic ice cream pails filled up fast. The foam bubbled at the top. New milk, never seen before.

We talked of life. The important things. It's not that we always necessarily agreed, but that we were sharing each other's thoughts. So many miles kept us apart most of our lives and here we were but for a few short minutes clinging to this time like rare morsels of the most precious of gems.

I listened intently, sensing all that made him feel the way he did. The experiences of a lifetime were pictured in my mind. His gentle laugh, his simple smile. All earth's glory and gain could not compare. No need to impress or be impressed. I felt as if I were his only friend. The hard world that ignored him. So I would take his thoughts and cherish them. Not let them fade. Nor let them be without purpose. I would let them be a part of me.

My words were of young exuberance. Developing thoughts, shaping a world.

Realizing our short time, we clung to the thoughts that mattered most.

The milking done. The cow at rest. The kittens asleep. The light turned off. The gate secured. The sun gone down. The cold settled in. And we walked hand in hand, each carrying a pail of milk. The yard light shone on the path before us. Through the yard and up to the little house. As we went inside to the folks who loved us, our time together closed as we shut the door. And the separations since are almost more than I can bear.

And now he sits, unable to walk. History written, time passed.

The sun still sets on that little shed. No cow to milk. No kittens to play. No one to protect from the chilling night air. And my heart yearns to see him. To walk down that road again, hand in hand, each carrying a pail of milk.

Written by Karen Stroebel

Berry Picking

LIFE IN THE RIVER VALLEY was not always without some recreational relief. During summers, when home full time, my parents would find a way for a few hours of recreation. Sometimes we would go visit my grandparents or just go for a Sunday drive and buy an ice cream cone, not a weekly trip, but an occasional one. Sometimes we would make it to the mission church for their Sunday services, but were never consistent. The most memorable times would be when mother and I would venture out on berry picking trips. Berry picking trips were a very important event for her. These trips also were a contributing source for our winter fruit reserve. These escapes provided a badly needed break from all the ranch activity, respite time, and to mother, nothing more enjoyable.

Mother and I had gone to a horse auction, purchasing a mare who was green broke, hauling her home in our pick-up. I worked with her for numerous days until she seemed to accept her training. Thinking that distances would be involved getting to and from a berry field, we decided to take this mare along as well as another one for mother to ride.

We piled all of our camping equipment into the cargo space atop the pickup's cab. Our equipment consisted of a tent, blankets, some food supplies, grain for the horses, and tack. We needed enough supplies to last about a week. Of course, our border collie had to go too, riding in the cab with us with the assigned job of keeping the bears away. Mother would never go berry picking without her dog. Bears were known for their love of berries and mother was convinced there would be one in every patch.

Selma J. Stroebel

These trips were like a mini-vacation for mother. Being relieved of all responsibility was a treat, giving a sense of freedom that seldom presented itself. She preferred to let me do the driving providing her with a sense of extended respite. According to Alberta law, I could drive as long as I was with a licensed driver even though I was under sixteen. By this time in my life, I had managed to rack up a number of driving hours, whether it was the family truck or my father's old case tractor. Anywhere mother wanted to go, I was always the driver. I had gained confidence in my driving skills as I had already driven under many different conditions. Deep snow, mud, rain, and snow storms as well as a loaded truck hauling horses; all had given me some driving challenges. By this time in my life I felt undaunted by it all.

Mother had decided the best potential for good berry picking was in the foothills of the Rockies. Highland cranberries and wild blueberries grew in the higher elevations, especially where jack pines were found. The closer we got to the foothills, chances were better for getting what she wanted.

Now being loaded, we were ready for take- off, so to speak. I don't exactly remember the roads which we traveled, but I do remember the dirt roads and the James River we had to ford. There would be no bridge to use for crossing this mountain stream. We would have to navigate through it. This fast moving flow of glacier fed water originated up somewhere higher in the mountains. There would be large river rocks to navigate over and around. Knowing that ahead of time really did not bother me; however, I had never driven under those conditions before with a load of horses, so I did give it a second thought.

Mainly hermits live up in those areas, usually a bachelor living like a mountain man who does not want to deal with life surrounded by anything that resembles civilization. Going up into wild country where few people live, makes you feel like you are on an exploration trip all by yourself. The independent spirit has to take control to deal with any problems that may occur. Your own ingenuity becomes your traveling companion.

Silent Tears

Going into the forest land untamed by man, was always an exhilarating experience and has a way of purifying the soul. Life in the woods seems simple, clean, pure, unspoiled by life's challenges. The virgin forest helps to remind you that much has gone on before your personal life ever began. There is an eternalness which you feel in this environment. The Bible refers to the fact that we can believe in and know the surety of an existence of God by the things which He has created. I look at a tree and say to myself, no man ever made that. I'm also reminded how comforting it is to know that Someone much greater than me exists and is in the process of working out His plan for our world. Revealing Himself through His Creation declares an omnipotence that boggles the mind of man. God also says in His Letter to mankind, that He has given us enough information about Himself through the things which He has made, for us to come to a belief in the one and only Almighty. Through His handiwork, God also declares that we will not be able to claim excuses for not believing. His love story to us is the greatest story ever told. Seeking to know Him as our life's priority, amazing discoveries unfold in very unexpected ways; otherwise our lives are diminished from what they could be, and missing out on those God whispers.

Heading westward to the foothills and mountains kept that magical pull going for us. We eventually came to the point where we needed to ford the river. Arriving at that point we noticed other traffic had gone before us recently, as wet tire tracks were evident on the exit side of the water. This gave us the confidence to approach this fast moving stream. The water was clear and we could easily see the bottom with all of those big rocks that averaged the size of two baseballs melded together. Some were smaller and some were larger, a few large enough that I wanted to totally miss them with my wheels. The depth of the stream seemed to be about eighteen to twenty four inches. This was the max of depth which we would want to deal with. If it rained, we would have to find another way out. The width of the stream was about fifty feet or more.

After carefully taking in all of the circumstances of that moment, I carefully and slowly approached the river's edge, hoping that this fording would go well. I would have to keep my foot lightly on the accelerator and steadily keep the truck moving forward until we reached the other side. Stopping in mid stream would not be ideal with all those rounded river rocks covering the bottom and the fast flowing water. Reaching the opposite river's edge was a big relief. If something had gone wrong there was no cell phone to call for help. They hadn't even been invented yet. However, life seemed to function quite well without them. We didn't know any better and had never learned to rely on that modern convenience. We didn't feel insecure with not having one either. When a problem came up we were used to figuring it out, somehow. That was the way life worked.

Continuing on down the forestry road with different species of trees lining the road's edge on either side, mother began to watch. She was looking for those jack pines which would indicate where either cranberries or blueberries were sure to be found. Eventually she found her spot, believing there were lots of possibilities. We were literally in the middle of nowhere. Many miles back, we had left behind any evidence of civilization. Only dirt trails lay ahead of us, but they too soon faded into only grassy trails. Nothing much existed except for forest land.

We unloaded our pickup and pitched our tent in the middle of this nowhere. We hobbled our horses to graze. Hobbling would keep them from wandering very far off. They could easily be located in the morning. Also preparing our sleeping facilities, eating something and all the while taking in our natural surroundings, we finally just went to bed.

Sleeping in this bottomless tent, with no air mattress was not a comfortable sleep by any one's imagination. All we had were some blankets separating our bodies from the hard ground. Waking up in the morning was like recovering from a drug overdose. Trying to get shut eye under those conditions did not provide a restful night's sleep. On previous trips we had tried laying pine branches on the ground first, then covering them with blankets.

Silent Tears

It was our method for trying to provide some kind of natural cushioning. The result of our experiment was natural cushioning does not work.

Next morning, after mother woke up bright-eyed and bushy-tailed, she returned to camp after doing her morning scouting of the area. After our breakfast of peanut butter and bread along with spring water we brought with us, she was ready to move. She thought there might be a good berry picking site down a trail she had spotted during her morning wanderings. She had sighted some trees which were a good indicator. This was the middle of August and the timing was right if good growing conditions existed during the earlier part of the season.

Mother had returned from her wanderings mentally ready to head out in hot pursuit. The idea of berry picking drew her like a magnet is drawn to a metal surface. She had inherited this magnetism from her father, only his magnet drew him to his sport of fishing. Dreaming of spending the day fishing along a trout stream was a drink of pure adrenaline. The idea of berry picking or going fishing always put them both in the hurry mode.

We had not built a campfire because of too much vegetation around us. We didn't want to be guilty of carelessly starting a forest fire. There was no evidence of anyone having had a previous campfire in the immediate area. There were no stone fire circles so we had decided to be on the safe side. There was too much short vegetation that could pose a real threat from fire sparks igniting nearby grass. However, a nice warm campfire in this morning's crispy cool mountain air would have been a real comfort.

We did not dismantle our campsite before leaving as we would plan to return later. We gathered together our berry picking equipment, tacked up the horses, and rode off down mother's discovered trail not knowing where this trail would eventually lead us. We assumed we would be riding a distance before actually finding a worthwhile berry patch.

Our berry picking equipment included aluminum five gallon pails tied to the front of the saddle. Mother had also made hand-held berry pickers.

She had soldered three inch nails to half an edge of an empty vegetable tin. These went along being carried in the pails. They worked very well pulling berries off short, fine-stemmed vines. In a good berry patch, you could fill a couple of five gallon pails in one morning or an afternoon.

Even though my horse was green broke, she was behaving very well. When they are in an unfamiliar environment a horse becomes dependent on you since they feel insecure in their new circumstances.

I said she was doing very well until we had stopped for our first picking. My back was turned toward her but out of the corner of my eye I could see and also hear my horse taking off at high speed down our just traveled trail. The saddle was totally turned, now underneath her belly instead of atop of her back. Apparently, the girth had become too loose to maintain its proper position. I had not double checked it's tightness after initially tacking up. Her quick exit suddenly ended our first picking stop and I'm thinking to myself, no telling how far this horse is going to go before we find her.

Surprisingly, it didn't take us very long to discover she had given up on the run of her life. After speeding about three quarters a mile down the trail we found her standing under a tree. The reins were tight against her mouth, the saddle turned and completely underneath her belly along with a very dejected facial expression. This total look of defeat was saying to me, "I really need your help." Straightening out the tack situation changed her countenance of desperation to a look of complete relief. I learned animals can be very expressive without any verbage. Their body language can say so much.

After that exciting incident, mother and I managed to fill our pails with blueberries before the end of the day. That night we had blueberry sandwiches along with some of that famous head cheese mother insisted on getting from the deli.

On berry picking trips we were never without a sandwich filler. Head cheese was a staple along with whatever berries we were picking that day.

Drinks were of the simple stuff, just plain old spring water toted in either glass jars or an old tin syrup pail. Sometimes spring water would be available from a mountain stream, but not always.

Our week stay was shortened by a couple of days with the arrival of rainy weather. After several days of the very pleasant sunny stuff and comfortable temperatures, we were ready to break camp now that the barometer was falling. The whole weather pattern was changing quickly. Those pleasant summer temperatures had taken their leave, replacing themselves with that piercing cold wet mountain air, the kind that goes through to the bone regardless of what you are wearing.

By the time we had taken down our tent, loaded up all of our gear, along with the horses in the pick-up, we were wet and cold. But we still had to get out of the forest land.

The road out was going to be different than the road in. The river would become too deep and dangerous to ford. Our other option was to take the high foothill shelf road going up a steep grade with a drop-off on the outside. The kind of drop off that makes you keep your eyes on the inside bank not letting them wander anywhere else. Not only would this one way narrow road be steep, but now with the rain it could be slippery with minimal gravel to help.

Meeting another motorist on this one way road involved cooperation on the part of both drivers. One of them would have to stop and wait, edging over to the inside as far as possible allowing the other driver to slowly inch by. Now if you happened to be the lucky one going downhill, waiting and passing wasn't so challenging. It was when you were the one going up the steep grade, plus dealing with the rainy weather road conditions and that steep incline on the outer edge, was when that emotional challenge grabbed your spirit. Since we no longer had a choice with the rainy weather having made that decision for us, our path out was going to be a drive up that shelf road with the pick-up loaded with a couple horses.

Selma J. Stroebel

This particular driving experience gave this teenage driver a lesson about awareness. Learning to drive under many different conditions and sometimes difficult conditions is a maturing process. The lesson learned that day was to know your conditions and act accordingly. Going slow and steady helped avoid any sliding due to wet mud and keeping eyes on that inside rock wall helped to keep a focus off the steep drop off. That day my driving skills matured to another level with an emotional pang, but not panic being a part of the scene.

Arriving back at the farm, we unloaded the pickup, let the horses back out to pasture, and took comfort around our wood burning space heater. We were soaked to the skin with wet clothes from that cold mountain rain. My brain felt like it was no longer going to function and my whole body was feeling stiff. Being able to be inside around our wood stove that radiated welcomed heat, felt so comforting. I had become so chilled from that wet mountain air, I felt as though I would never be warm again. That, of course, was an illusion of the mind. I think I now understand what hypothermia feels like.

The next morning with the sunshine in full bloom and a cloudless sky, we were feeling renewed and reenergized after the big wet chill. Now it was time to clean those berries. A slight breeze provided a mild movement of air and was just about right for berry cleaning. The air movement has to be just enough to fan the fruit in separating them from the small leaves. Too much wind and the berries blow away along with the leaves. Mother's method of using the natural movement of a gentle breeze proved to be an efficient and easy method for cleaning.

She would go to the closet and get the largest bed sheet available, then take it outside and spread it on top of the lawn's short grass. Holding a bucket of berries as high over her head as possible, she would begin to very slowly pour the berries onto the sheet below, waiting for a gentle breeze to fan the leaves. Mother called this technique "winding the berries". Using this kind of breeze would methodically and easily separate the leaves from the fruit. Sometimes she would repeat the process several times with the same bucket full to completely remove the green foliage. This method saved us a lot of work. After repeating this process until all the buckets had been winded, came the last step which was the water bath. This was simply pouring water into the buckets of berries and swishing them around to remove any residue.

Mother now considered them to be ready for canning. After all of the different steps: packing, traveling, camping, searching for a berry patch, dealing with the weather, cleaning, and then the last step of canning, they would finally become part of the fruit inventory for the winter season. In the middle of that icy season, these berries provided some warm weather memories along with a very refreshing flavor, which was a nice addition to the limited fruits available in cold climate grocery stores.

These occasions allowed for some mother-daughter time, something that we didn't have much of. These times spent together were positive, memorable, and a time where we could feel free-spirited.

Social Life in the River Valley

ATTENDING AUCTIONS on nearly a weekly basis, involved time and energy that drained any impetus for a variable social life. Neither of my parents sought an active outside connection with others. Most associations were related someway to their farming business or church attendance. Community involvement was non-existent except to vote. Neighbor contact was limited, except for one neighbor and his wife of German descent who lived on an adjacent quarter section of land. Their proximity to my parent's property facilitated occasional contact.

Dutch, a nickname, and his wife, liked to come unannounced for a visit. Being semi retired, sleeping until noon was a privilege they could afford, but not my parents. Knocking on our door shortly after the dinner hour in mid-evening, usually staying till daylight started to break the following morning, you realized immediately that a lengthy visit was in store. Community news, political subjects, stories from the old country mixed with some jokes he liked to tell, were subjects of conversation all being shared around some sweet treat mother would try to provide. Neither of my parents was confrontational enough to suggest leaving earlier might be a good idea so your host could get some sleep before the new day started. Our family had morning chores that started early, so sleeping late was not a privilege we could enjoy.

My parents enjoyed their company, providing the listening ear, while Dutch did most of the talking expressing his thoughts on life direct and to the point. It was through him that my mother learned of the rumor being spread by my father's parents of my mother driving my father crazy.

Coyote Annie, an acquaintance of Mother's, was an attractive, tall, blonde, middle-aged Dutch lady with long hair. She was an immigrant like most other Canadians who had come from European countries many years prior. She still spoke with a strong accent but was very understandable in her speech. I have to mention this rarity of a personality because of her uniqueness and, also finding her to be intriguing.

She had long, blonde hair that came midway down her back as well as possessing a physical beauty which could easily have made it possible for her to enter a beauty contest in another environment.

This day of our introduction through my mother, Coyote Annie was wearing worn and faded denim overalls topped with a traditional red plaid flannel shirt usually found on a man's back. Her presence aura made her appear to ready for any kind of outdoor duty. However, her persona didn't seem to fit in with this isolated environment. As I studied her while being in her presence, I came to the conclusion that she had located herself into this remoteness for economical reasons; available and affordable. This was an understandable logic.

Living within this vale surrounded by high forested foothills in the shadow of the Rockies, still seemed very remote for this tall attractive blond with persona plus. Upon arriving and greeted with a friendly and welcoming smile, we were given a quick tour. She was obviously happy to have some visitors which I would say did not happen that often in this remoteness. She did appear to have a live-in companion who seemed to function more within the role of a drone. I'm well aware that appearances don't tell the whole story.

However, here she was living a hermit-like lifestyle totally isolated from any kind of civilization. The closest store was located on a very winding road leading downward from her ranch to a much lower altitude. This trip was very scenic during the warm weather seasons, but a much different kind of drive with snow covered roads and hidden black ice conditions, challenging the best of drivers. This nearest store was not just around the bend, but many miles around many bends that could be a winter's nightmare trip.

The negatives which I have just stated can easily be erased by the beauty of her home's setting. Her slab constructed house was nestled on the northern edge of a beautiful vale, surrounded by foothills dressed in emerald evergreens creating nature's picture that wholly cradled her ranch. A beautiful meadow surrounded the slab built outbuildings providing a contrast with the hilly background. A picture perfect setting, a rare scene to behold, a feast for the eyes, and a tranquilizer for the soul.

She and her companion had accomplished a lot to enhance the property. Several slab outbuildings that existed were plentifully adorned with cow head skeletons and wild life antlers. Pole fences stretched long distances to define boundaries. Wildlife hides also adorned her home's interior. A bear skin rug including the head lay on the floor next to her bed. Another bear skin without the head covered the bed being used as a blanket. Throughout this slab house other hides adorned the rough hewn wood floor. It was obvious that wildlife had provided them with meat and the remains had been used for adornment. This gave a completely new flavor to interior design and décor.

Legend had given her the name of "Coyote Annie," due to a personal story regarding the lifestyle which she lived. She had adopted an orphaned coyote pup, tying it to her kitchen table leg while keeping it in her house, tentatively raising it into adulthood, then returning the mature coyote back to its wild environment. Thus, she was crowned with the name.

Coyote Annie was a self-proclaimed veterinarian. This had been the reason for our visit from the beginning. Mother had two young tomcats she wished to have neutered. This request from my mother had come while I was on one of my summer visits. There was a distance to drive from my mother's residence to Annie's, plus mother was in the mood for a motor trip through the countryside. My father was no longer living and mother had left behind her career days of animal care. Both goals could be accomplished at the same time.

We were at this high foothill ranch for little over an hour, being introduced to this unique person, having a guided tour, exchanging stories, and acting like we had known each other for years. The final act, a quick identity change of these two toms, ended our visit. Let me say it this way, she knew how to get the job done in the bat of an eye, with the help of her companion of course.

Our visit with this unique personality and the guided tour of rarity was over, but fond mental pictures have remained.

Our social life in essence was always connected to farm business one way or another. Auction mart days, trips for supplies, or infrequent church attendance, seemed to be the regulars of our social life in the summer. There would be other events that showed up on the calendar infrequently. Going to a local stampede, attending the local fair maybe, and also those fishing trips with my grandfather brought some variety to our lives. These trips with him were a highlight. A dearth of social connection with friends during the summer was an outlet that just did not exist.

Mother and I never went on mother-daughter shopping trips together. Apparel needs were ordered from either Sears Roebuck catalogue or Eaton's, (a Canadian mail order company). Any order always took a week to fill and receive.

Birthdays never included a big celebration like it does in some families. On your birthday morning the acknowledgement would be a verbal, "Today is your birthday, happy birthday," and then followed by a hug with nothing more stated.

Holidays received much more recognition as a focus for the family. Christmas Day was always something we looked forward to as that day was usually spent at either my grandparent's house or at my uncle's place. A large roasted turkey adorned a platter on the dining room table with my grandfather wielding his carver's knife and fork, asking each of us what part of the turkey we wanted. I remember always asking for the tail. As an adult I can't image why the tail was such a coveted piece of meat but as a child it was my favorite.

Farms are known for their demands on a person's time with little left for recreation. This was particularly true for my parents and their concept of time management. When I was home during the summer, a Sunday afternoon drive and a stop for an ice cream cone, a visit to my grandparent's home, an occasional visit to the mission church, or the annual local stampede competition which I attended with my aunt and uncle was the extent of our social life. My parents never made an effort to attend those local competitive events.

After I left home and moved to Wisconsin, mother became the mission church pianist and also planned events for the young people. She did not see much happening for them so decided to get involved. With the farm now downsized, even though she was in her seventies and enjoyed her music, she decided to use that as a connection to the youth in this small country church. She learned how to construct kazoos by using a toy kazoo and soldering it to tin cans of different sizes to amplify the sound. She made one for each member of the group. The youth loved her effort and that also brought a big sparkle to her eyes earning the nickname "Bright Eyes" Getting involved with the youth was an energizing drive for late in life goal orientation. Productive use of time was always what mother was about even into her nineties.

More and more I looked forward to the times I would be spending away from home. Time away gave a reprieve from my parents constant arguing which usually involved mother doing the talking while my father listened without giving any response.

As I would listen to the verbal monologue after being away from home for many weeks; why did I even bother to come home would cross my mind. The positive environment of living with other families or being at boarding school was not enough to keep me from spiraling downward emotionally. The long steep slide down had been inching slowly. I was stepping into a black hole with no bottom and no way out. I was doing everything I knew to do to hide my condition. I felt mother had enough problems to deal with, and after all she was depending on me for her emotional support.

Mother's unhappiness and my father's dysfunction without answers were having an accumulative destructive effect. Their emotional needs, especially my mother's, had become a controlling factor in my life. Her needs became my focus and my needs were not allowed to cross my mind. I blocked them out. In reality, I was in my own dysfunctional state. Verbalizing my own needs was something I never gave any thought. All of my thought energy was directed in my parent's direction. Instead of focusing on what I needed to do for myself, my focus became trapped inside of their dysfunction. Intervention by an outside force did not exist.

I passed off my parent's non-attendance to my graduation as something I was not going to think about. Instead, I was going to return to the farm and help mother as I owed it to her, but in the end it was a huge mistake. The depth of my parent's problems gave me no hope for any kind of solutions. I came to the conclusion that only death could solve their problems. I had now become very discouraged for them while, in the meantime, my own emotional well-being was sinking to new lows. Life was no longer worth living. My downward spiral was speeding up. I was unable to think in terms of any hope or avenues for getting psychological help, a term that I was not familiar with at that time.

Making the decision to go back to school came from the feeling of being destroyed; the push to leave or else. I had to leave. I am being destroyed, I thought. Being filled with desperation and anxiety during the beginning of that fall school term was also the time I prayed asking God to, "please heal my mind, I don't like the way I am." In my mind there were no other options available and a tough year lay ahead.

That autumn I met my future husband, and little did I know that God would not only answer my prayer, but also bring across my life's path much needed information. It was much more than I anticipated, leading me into badly needed information and understanding of my father's problems. God's answer to my prayer was much broader than I had expected or hoped for. Eventually the information led me to not only understand my father, but also other family circumstances. God knew what I needed for real emotional healing to take place when of course I did not have a clue. Nor did I ever dream that His answer would be revealed to me over such an extended period of time. A lot of dots had to appear before I was able to start connecting them.

I had three areas in my life that needed healing. First, my own dysfunctional emotional state was badly in need of repair. The condition in which

I had become was now so severe that my ability to help anyone else was beyond my capability. I needed peace in my life. Second, I needed to have some peace regarding my mother's unhappiness. Thirdly, I needed some understanding of my father. Why was he the way he was? He had become a nonperson to me as a daughter. He was a human being with very little personality. I had never had a single meaningful conversation with this man. My own validation was a big question in my mind and remained that way until I was able to seek out some answers for myself.

As my healing began to take place, some understanding regarding my mother began to form as well. I could not be the source of her happiness. That was a thought that I could intellectualize, but emotionally unable internalize. Totally rising above that did not occur until her passing. I had grieved for her so much while she was living that I didn't miss her when she was gone. I had already done my grieving, and I was emotionally spent. With her passing my silent tears had come to an end. My mother was now at peace in her heavenly home.

What has remained? Some large regrets linger for my mother's sake. If only she could have understood the real problem of my father's condition. Life for her could have been a lot less complex. Perhaps our family life could have been more cohesive and orderly. My father could have received the understanding which he so rightly deserved.

However, the highway we travel called life, is a journey with a beginning at birth and ends with that stepping stone we take into our eternal reward for the life lived in between. All of life lived in between these two posts are a preparation for the home God has planned for us. Learning to live life with eternity in view is a daily task of setting truly valuable priorities. A problem, that becomes a real challenge, sometimes causes us to live with mysteries that are difficult to explain defying simple answers.

Piecing Together a Puzzle

September---1986

"I'M NOT CONVINCED that your father has Parkinson's disease." This statement was made to me personally during a conference which I had requested with my father's doctor.

A different physician had diagnosed my father with Parkinson's Disease (PD) a few years prior, due to his overall failing health, and I had taken this as fact. Since I was rarely present, my brother took on the responsibility of seeing that my parents received the medical treatment they needed.

During this conference with my father's doctor, he went on to describe the symptoms in detail of this disease. My father's present symptoms had caused this doctor to question this former diagnosis, as my father had some of them, but not enough major ones to confirm. The image I had of my father from the previous year didn't fit the described symptoms either. He had easily peddled a stationary bike without any stiffness in his limbs. This would be difficult for a PD patient to perform, as his doctor described.

I had flown from Milwaukee to Alberta that autumn, after receiving a call from mother. She related that my father was in the hospital, very ill, and maybe would not survive much longer. She asked me, "Please come home, you may never see your father again." I proceeded to reserve an emergency flight with United Airlines into Calgary, meeting my brother who picked me up, then headed directly to the hospital.

Silent Tears

My mother informed me that my father had a lot of chest congestion, plus some other issues which elude my memory. My parents were always having emergencies of one kind or another so I didn't let myself internalize too many details beyond the obvious. However, the issue of his Parkinson's Disease was certainly part of his health picture in our minds.

My father had already been in the hospital for a number of days and nothing seemed to be changing, however, a real concern remained. Family members would come and go making the usual visits. Mother and I spent endless hours at the hospital, since that was where she wanted to be. I passed the time with a knitting project. The creativity helped to keep my mind occupied and distracted while waiting for changes to take place. Also, this slowed down time capsule gave me some one on one time with mother, time which we rarely had. I wanted to be an emotional support for her. She had dearly missed that we no longer lived in Alberta. When my husband and I moved, she was completely convinced that she would never see us again.

Spending this lengthy time at the hospital, that had turned into a couple of weeks with little change in my father's condition, spurred my intention for a private medical consultation one on one. As the doctor proceeded to describe the symptoms of Parkinson's and the effect it has on the patient, he also spoke of his doubt regarding my father's former diagnosis. After listening to his description, I became doubtful as well. Most of the symptoms relating to PD which he described were not ones apparent in my father's current condition. It was also obvious this doctor had given this subject a great deal of thought to declare his disbelief with the original diagnosis. After this consultation, I proposed this doubt to my family members but they remained adamant with the original PD diagnosis.

After spending three weeks in the hospital, my father was released into mother's care. I returned to Milwaukee with information in my head that I had not considered before. This professional opinion kept stirring in my mind; there had to be some answers somewhere. In my mind, I had excused much of his behavior to the onset of PD, perhaps beginning many, many years prior. Not that this disease could cause all of his problems, but it gave an excuse for such behavior where no other excuses existed. Now that PD had been removed from the picture, that opened the door for some other considerations and possibilities. The years gone by could be re-thought and reviewed.

I was feeling confident with the doctor's opinion. He was so specific in his details. He was bringing some real clarity to the picture in one sense, yet creating another mystery. We still had no real answers. This doctor knew I wanted to know and understand what was going on with my father. I appreciated the time he gave explaining his theory.

He mentioned that seventy percent of patients with PD have tremors. My father had none. He also spoke of how the muscles in a PD patient lose their flexibility and stiffness occurs. My father displayed only minor stiffness through a shuffled walk, but at the age of eighty-two that was not abnormal. He was able to ride a stationary bike, peddling with quite apparent flexibility, only forgetting to keep peddling so had to be reminded. As a family, we had observed him riding his stationary bike with plenty of flexibility in his legs six months prior to his hospitalization.

I needed some answers now more than ever. With this doctor's opinion I had new information to consider. This large cavern of dysfunction had so negatively affected our family and my own emotional health causing me to lose my drive for life and blocking out mentally that which I did not want to take in. At times, mother's unhappiness was almost unbearable. She deserved much more in life than she was getting. It had to be more than, "The devil makes him do these things," according to my mother.

I felt driven to watch for clues which could provide some insights. Something inside me was saying "There is more to this picture, keep searching." The problem was I did not know where to look. Perhaps just watching, as days come and go, clues would eventual surface. And they did, but it was going to take time and maturity on my part.

Sometime within the following year of my father's hospitalization, I had turned on the television set, tuning in for a diversion from whatever I was doing. The program being aired at that hour was related to how head injuries can cause Parkinson's like symptoms. A famous boxer was a guest on the show, claiming that his head injuries from boxing had caused him to develop these PD symptoms. My mental response was, "Hmm, that is interesting."

This caused me to recall a statement which mother had made to me as a child, a statement made with no place to hang the thought. It was nothing more than a memory tucked away in my brain, with no associations made with it. At the time there was no reason to attach any significance, especially to this child's mind. In fact, I have wondered why I even remembered it. I could not have been more than a five year old at the time.

Mother had made reference to my father as a six-year -old, helping my grandfather's hired men install fencing on the ranch. The hired man missed the post with the post maul, instead hitting my father on the head, knocking him unconscious for some time. I never heard anyone else make any references to the accident. Hers was the only one. My father apparently told my mother about the accident otherwise she would never have known. How much he remembered regarding the situation is a question that will remain unanswered.

This fencing accident had received no further acknowledgements in any manner. Until I was demonstrating how to clip my father's hair by using the new electric hair clipper. A demonstration request had been made by mother. She had always used the old-fashioned hand clipper; however, her arthritic hands could no longer perform that task, so she requested an electric one. "Please bring one with you when you visit next time," was her request. As I was demonstrating with this new clipper, I noticed a ridge around my father's head. I thought to myself, this is what mother talked about. She had never wanted my father to get a barber's hair cut as they cut it so short the ridge around his head showed and she didn't like that. Also, as I was demonstrating how to use this appliance, I noticed a definite indentation in his skull, above his right ear. Due to so many years between being told of the accident and the use of the clippers revealing these physical evidences, I was unable to make any conscious connections between what I had been told and what I was visibly seeing. At this point in time I was still not connecting any dots.

Thinking that I was only demonstrating hair cutting with a new gadget, I realized that I was seeing something I had never seen before. This indentation, which was large enough to place a couple of finger pads within, along with his physical ridge, was now registering in my mind. It occurred to me they were related to that accident many years ago when he was a child. Although I was seeing this physical evidence, I still did not connect this to his personality traits. I finished my demonstration. Mother was happy with the results of her new hair clippers. With the demo completed, a different discussion entered into the conversation and I never made any comments to mother regarding my observations.

Upon mother's death, I was helping to prepare her house for resale. Through the process, I came across a medical and x-ray report of my father's, dated thirty-eight years prior to my father's death. The report revealed a brain adhesion, no treatment was suggested and a follow up visit was not scheduled. I do remember that he suffered a lot of headaches. This medical examination was probably instigated because of them. I did not retain the report, something which I regret, still lacking the knowledge of its significance. I had become so fed up with our family and all the unsolvable problems; I felt the strong need to declare an end. Both of my parents were now deceased. I so wanted this story to be finished.

I still had not been able to compile in my mind, clues and symptoms leading to a comprehensible diagnosis. Clues had presented themselves over a very long period of time. Piecing them together, did not come until the concept of a closed head injury presented itself in a medical article. An article which I just happened to pick up in a random act. Anyway, at the time I thought this act was a random act, but later I changed my mind.

The information presented in the medical article, along with library and internet research on a closed head injury, I became thoroughly convinced that this was my father's problem all along. No one in the family had a clue. My mother certainly did not connect my father's behavior to this early childhood accident. Nor do I believe his family did.

The symptoms clearly described my father. His shuffling feet as he walked, his frozen facial muscles when he opened his mouth to ha, ha, ha, in laughter at a joke were symptomatic of PD, but had been somewhat misleading in his former diagnosis. His eyes did not light up with a normal brightness when laughing nor did his smile muscles frame a smile. These were indicators of PD; however, all of these symptoms are also symptomatic of a closed head injury. These characteristics, so obvious to my present mind, but so totally missed in the past.

Beyond these obvious characteristics were the memory behaviors, the cognitive difficulties, the many migraine headaches which he suffered, the lack of ability for oral communication and concentration. He had a constant need for sleep as well. Again, all of these combined are evidences of a closed head injury. This also explains why routine was my father's friend, a safety net for him. Predictability made his day much more organized without any need for planning or trying to solve complex problems or remembering to complete a task. Now his behaviors were finally explainable.

As my father aged, these characteristics became more obvious when I look back with a more informed mind. The hallucinations which he suffered also became more frequent toward the closing years of his life.

I now comprehend to a much fuller degree the stresses my mother had to deal with. The strength of her character was displayed through her perseverance, determination, hard work, and intelligence. Her under-lying faith in a loving heavenly Father, believing that He would provide a way, was the sustaining foundation to her life. Because of this, she determined to never be a quitter, never stopping short of a personal goal. Even the last few months of my father's bedridden life, when she was in her early eighties, she determined to care for him with no outside help

Unfortunately, no one in the family was able to connect any dots during my parent's lifetime. Medical research on the brain was just not there yet. Now I am able to connect events that create a sensible conclusion for my father's condition, dispelling earlier false assumptions. It would be reasonable for my father's parents to believe my mother was driving their son crazy. Not having any medical input to explain their son's seemingly irrational behavior, they now had a visible excuse for explaining it away. Since they were social status conscious, his problems were not a family problem, but someone else's fault.

During the beginning years of my parent's marriage, I believe the breakdown between father and son became permanently broken. This successful father could not accept a son who performed far below his expectations. The result: he fired his own son and my father was unable to defend himself. My father's lack of normal developmental changes as a child was camouflaged by the uniqueness of each child's development. For his family, this is the way he always was. Small daily changes are hard to recognize due to familiarity. However, my ability to give his parents the complete benefit of doubt is a stretch. I am convinced that my father's lack of performance skills became more evident as he matured and with his family being status conscious, my mother provided an explainable excuse for my father's underperformance. I am convinced as well, they truly believed mother was driving their son crazy, never connecting his behaviors to the closed head injury he had received as that six year old child.

Since they believed that my mother was driving their son crazy, the action in which they tried to take our home away from us, giving us three days in which to move a whole farm, has a little bit of logic behind it. Since his father and mother were in their mid-seventies, having that plot of land go to their son with a wife who was driving their son crazy, believing he would be unable to manage it, was not acceptable in their minds. They certainly would not want my mother to gain control of something which they valued. After all, she was the one driving their son crazy. They had miscalculated my mother's fighting will.

The illogical aspect of their request exposed itself by thinking a whole farm, livestock, machinery, and household items could be moved in three days? Another aspect presented the question of, where would we move to? Did that actually mean they were willing to put us on the road, as in homeless? These are dots that I have not been able to connect. Also, why was my grandfather not willing to give his own grandson even an apple? After all, the apple was not going to diminish his wealth much.

Without ever having the opportunity to meet or have a conversation with my grandparents, I try to understand their character by the lives they lived, coming to the conclusion social standing was a driving force, success in business and money brought the status they desired not wanting that image to be tarnished. Generosity was not a part of my grandfather's character. Giving of himself in a selfless way was not a trait he had learned. Maybe sometimes, I think, I am being too generous in my spirit toward my father's parents.

This family history of such poor relationships has profoundly influenced me. This cycle of relationships I did not want to be a part of repeating. Learning a lot of what not to do, I wondered if he ever gave his personal legacy any consideration. I can only project these questions into his mind without any hope of having any answers.

Imagining the reaction which my father's family had as he revived from his unconscious state was probably one of relief and thinking now they have their son back. Feeling that everything was now going to be okay. Little did they know the extent of the physical injury and the consequences that would result or how near a death state he had been in. When I review in my mind the physical evidence which I personally saw at the time of demonstrating a hair cut with the electric clipper, I marvel that he was not killed. No wonder he had cognitive problems. Also, there is no evidence that I can refer to that his family ever connected any dots that would enable them to understand their son, or brother.

The youth of children can have quick regenerative powers. Perhaps he was not much different immediately after his revival from the coma. His parents, were likely unaware that the head injury was affecting his cognitive and behavioral development. While continuing to grow physically, normal psychological development was likely interrupted, however, may have been undetectable to the casual observer. Trained professional medical resources were unavailable at the time.

"How could I have been so stupid?" This question my mother voiced but was more a statement she was making to herself. In my mind, I reword that question, in order to ask myself some other ones. What kept you from recognizing any cautionary signals while you were dating? How come you missed indicators of future problems? Were they not apparent?

Dating time and married life represent different periods in a couple's togetherness. I can visualize mother being the talkative one while my father sat quietly listening in a passive manner. His quiet persona probably made her feel safe. She had related to me numerous times how abuse had been prevalent in families. There were a couple of times when she articulated the thought that maybe her mother was not her real mother. Her brother seemed to be greatly favored during their growing years. This was emotional abuse in her mind, but never verbalized in this manner. However, I am convinced that my mother felt safe in dating my father. Her strong personality made her sensitive to one who would be bossy or had controlling tendencies. Those characteristics would have made her run in the other direction. Since those qualities did not seem apparent, she believed he was the one for her. If questionable behaviors surfaced on the part of my father, she probably denied their existence or the symptoms of his injury were still benign enough they could easily be explained away. After all, she was not a witness to his daily responsibilities while working on his father's ranch. Her only exposure to him was in the dating scene.

It is unfortunate for my parent's marriage that some dots were never connected. Instead of harmony, there was always arguing. Mother lived with the unrealistic dream that some day he would change, never grasping the concept that change would be impossible for him. My mother had expectations of her husband that were unrealistic, but how could she know that? Age and time had their degenerative powers, slowly creeping like a slow growing cancer into the very fibers of his personality. The adhesion which showed up on the x-ray probably had its unknown effect, especially without the ability for further diagnostic examination.

I now understand why we often had very little food on the table or clothes in the closet. Why the exterior of our house was bare of paint, portraying the tobacco row appearance. Why our home had no plumbing and was furnished with rough and worn furniture. Why our house was cold in the winter without central heat. (On summer visits, my husband installed plumbing, central heat, and built kitchen cabinets for my mother---All I can say to that is---Bless His Heart). My mind accepts the fact that I had to continuously check on my father to see if he was safe. I can see the reasons for mother's insecurities. I can understand her deep need to have someone listen, as she emotionally dumped on me as a child. She would reach the point where she was totally emotionally spent. Her emotional valve would erupt. She stated several times that I was all she had, a large load for an unequipped child to bear. I can also see more fully the intelligence which she possessed. Her bright mind and talents were far beyond mine.

The man in our family who was so misunderstood, living a life of quiet routine, quite unaffected and unaware of the conflict surrounding him, and unable to comprehend the turmoil in his family. When my mother would nag him, comprehension of the issues did not sink in. His indifference had been interpreted as not caring. In reality he was not able to care, living in a mental fog with his cognitive abilities severely interrupted. Unfortunately no one recognized that fact.

Believing that my father did not care for his family made me to not want to look him in the face. I had built up my own share of resentment and anger. After all, since I had never had a meaningful conversation with this man, he was a very unnecessary figure that really did not need to be around, totally not relating to each other. He brought no honor to the family, only a pack of problems. I had become very tired of our family scene, but ached for my mother shedding more silent tears, whenever she came to mind.

Peace Finally Comes

In the depths of my despondancy, my desperate prayer for mental and emotional healing, calling on the One of whom I believed to exist, and uttered as a momentary thought which I had at the moment with no concept of how an answer would come. A blank slate of possibilities rolled out before me like a long paved road that narrowed to a thread with the end disappearing into the far distant horizon.

Feeling like I was close to a complete emotional breakdown without options and trapped in my own mindset, that prayer was my only hope at the moment. My family was as dysfunctional as I was.

Prayer is an act that requires very little faith, something which I have discovered. The Bible says that if you have the faith of a mustard seed, you have faith. I understand that the mustard seed is the tiniest of all seeds. I had never practiced using prayer as a daily discipline. In boarding school we had our scheduled quiet times, but not personally chosen as a discipline. Prayer for me had not become a habit.

Realizing that I had to do something to save myself, I believed a change in focus was essential as I was emotionally spent. Signing up for those basic college courses brought the refocusing I was looking for. Even though it was a very difficult year emotionally, the college environment and meeting my future husband helped me experience a badly needed paradigm shift enabling me to seek recovery for myself. Now married, my allegiance was no longer to my mother and I was going to have to put her out of my mind even though she believed she would never see us again when we moved to Milwaukee. After all, her only emotional support was leaving the country and that was devastating to her.

Our move to Milwaukee was a huge transition in my life along with the years which followed. I could feel my recovery taking place, my spirit being renewed, but I still knew I had a long way to go to emotionally feel healthy. Through that conversation with Jim's doctor, it became clear to me there were changes I needed to make. Making that personal commitment to myself became revolutionary in my recovery. It was not long before I began to recognize how much recovery I was actually experiencing.

Reading books or pertinent medical reports related to the field of psychology and diligently seeking out information in order to broaden my knowledge in that field became great tools to bring insights. Spending time reading the Book of Proverbs brought many thoughts of wisdom and a sense of balance on how to live life. Also, during that whole process, I became impressed on how God has gifted extraordinary minds with the ability to study, research, and find insights on how the brain works there by bringing help to those of us who suffer with these maladies. The past couple of decades have experienced tremendous advances in the field of medicine. I also became impressed with the giftedness which God has given to minds in other fields that have benefited humanity. Science and modern day technology are mind boggling, with the exploration of space and how man was able to transport himself to the moon. The list could go on and on. I realize that there are abuses in every field, but they don't negate the positives coming from the many minds which God has blessed with superior intelligence.

Looking back over the journey traveled, a miracle had surely taken place in my life coming from many God orchestrated sources. Remembering the saga of my lengthy depression, the hopelessness which I felt, the lack of relationship with my father, the unhealthy one with my mother, the non-validation of my personhood, adds up to a dark time for a growing young adult. That lack of validation had its long term negative effect. The extended times away from home, when closeness of family life should be the norm, but seldom existed. I felt my family was a lost cause with no solutions that could provide even a glimmer of hope for their happiness, especially for my mother. I had been letting her unhappiness affect me deeply without setting boundaries, while my father was just a blah in my life. I had finally come to the conclusion that the only real solution for them would come through their own demise. Unfortunately, that conclusion proved to be true.

The length and depth of this rough journey did not diminish the appreciation and sacrifice my mother made for me. Her effort to keep me from being confined to the limits of our farm was truly visionary on her part. My time away, whether with other families or boarding school were difficult for both of us, but especially difficult for my mother to accept, however, enriching for me. It was a sacrifice for each of us, since we were both deprived of a close family relationship. She really missed our time together, while I just became more emotionally independent. This was an accusation tossed my direction quite a few times.

Yes, I had reached a level of satisfaction with my recovery from this long term depression that had lasted over a period of many years. I was feeling good about myself as I was sane and that spelled success to my mind. That definition for success is not one that is generally thought of as an acceptable one. However, that meaning is more appropriate than the usual definition because of what I have been through. My definition of that word usually causes a double take to the ear that is listening. Monetary and educational aspects are generally associated with that term, rather than sanity.

Even though my own psychological issues were being resolved within myself, I still had not reconciled my parents. I did not recognize that resolving their issues was needed for wholeness within myself until after they were gone to their heavenly home. Many more God whispers had to take place pushing me to understand I had not as of yet received complete emotional healing. Many God whispers had confronted my thinking, bringing insights to their dysfunctional lives and my own.

Connecting the dots of information which became apparent over an extended span of years was necessary to be able to come to terms with a life -long mystery. The medical knowledge also had to be available to support conclusions. Without the combination of it all, my father's true condition would never have been known.

His doctor questioning a former diagnosis of Parkinson's Disease, opened my mind to consider some other alternatives. The television program relating to head injuries opened the door for serious reconsideration of that which I had believed all along. The concept of a closed head trauma and its serious side effects had not been considered, until that moment. Totaling all this information, along with my personal research, I discovered the symptoms we were observing in my father's behavior were giving us enough information to ensure us of the real explanation for my father's condition. Having also had the opportunity, to personally observe the physical evidence of his skulls indentation and the apparent collapse of the skull cap causing the ring around his head, brought some conviction to my mind that we were finally on the right track for a convincing diagnosis. Knowing that my father was not mentally slow as a result of genetics, but had these characteristics because of an accident was relieving. He did not leave gates and doors open carelessly, it was that he would sincerely forget. He did care for his family through following his routines. He really was a warm person, trying to prove that through simple gestures, like saying "Thank you," when a deed was done. With all of his cognitive problems, the ability to show that you sincerely care for those close to you would be difficult to demonstrate.

We did not have a relationship with his family because he was unable to cope with its complexity. Since I never met or had a conversation with his parents, I have very little information to know what they were thinking during our days of living across the road from each other. This whole non relationship with close relatives that live across the road and are your closest neighbor draws a complete blank, in my mind.

I came to understand the complexities of life were beyond his ability to cope. Mother handled the business, the lawsuit, and daily details because that was all beyond his capability. Their abilities were so unequal. This fact was disturbing to me. Mother had so much talent and intelligence that was being consumed through a life of spinning its wheels.

This raises another question in my mind. If God walks before us directing our paths, how come God didn't protect my mother from making a decision that so negatively affected her life? On the other hand, where would my father be without the care which mother provided? What kind of a life would he be having? My questioning reminds me of the movie, "The Fiddler on the Roof," with Tevia doing his questioning regarding his daughters and their marriages. He would consider one idea and then say to himself, "On the other Hand" to consider another aspect of the situation. And that is where I have to leave these questions, with no concrete answers. However, I can be okay with that. I was not present when these decisions were made.

I greatly regret we did not have this knowledge during my father's lifetime. He was so greatly misunderstood by everyone around, including me. Like my mother, he deserved so much more respect and understanding, than what he received, and mother did not deserve being accused of driving my father crazy.

Being able to connect the dots that provided clues which had presented themselves over decades of time became a realization that I finally had resolved the mystery surrounding my father. I was the only one in our family who was able to bring any insights to this long standing saga of misconceptions. As a result I have been able to share these evidences with other members of my family, bringing relief to their minds as well. I greatly regret that these symptomatic clues were not connected during my father's lifetime. He deserved so much more respect than what he received.

The ability to link together the symptoms of a closed head injury, gave permission to dispel the family cloud, a truly liberating factor. Grasping the concept of this emotional liberation comes with a reminder of the earlier and simple prayer I had prayed as a twenty-one year old. God whispers and His orchestrating of events brought answers God knew I needed to finally have peace. Arriving at the point of being able to have personal peace after such a long personal struggle, brings a freedom of the spirit unmatched by anything that one could ever have.

The lengthy time span of several decades involved in God answering that short simple prayer, presents another question. Why did it take God so long to answer that prayer? I'm convinced my own emotional immaturity, the life experiences I needed, plus my grasp of the character of God, all had to be expanded before I could ever comprehend the miracle of God's personal involvement in bringing about His purposes in my life. His miracles can go unrecognized until we begin to recognize the puzzle pieces coming together to create the picture we are looking for, in my case, being able to solve the mystery surrounding my father. His unseen miracles are happening all around us with His purposes hard to grasp and sometimes never internalized.

A recognized miracle which took place involved my adult daughter and me on one of our visits to my mother's. We had just flown to Alberta to spend some time with family. Arriving at mother's residence, the usual catching up of news etc. was taking place. I was personally eyeing her rooms looking for changes and safety issues due to her age. Mother always had her Bible open and lying on her kitchen table so that she could read in short spurts due to her failing eyesight. As I took note of her table's contents my eyes fell unintentionally onto a verse which made reference to God protecting us from accidents. My mental reaction at that moment was, "Well, maybe so?" My mind left it all there with no further thought.

Time came for us to visit my niece in Red Deer. My uncle was willing to lend my daughter and me his pick-up for transportation during our ten day family visit. Using his truck, we headed for my niece's home to spend the day.

Having had a great visit with afternoon tea, as is the custom there, along with a hike to the local park, laughing and joking, we were simply enjoying our time together. Nighttime came with daylight fading quickly, rain moved in, and time to leave showed up on the clock.

As we were leaving the city lights, everything became much darker with a glare from our headlights giving mirror like reflections on the wet blacktop and falling rain drops. Visibility had become quite poor but still was able to maintain a fifty-five mile per hour speed limit. Just as we made our transition from city lights into this darkness and low visibility, instantly we both saw two huge images so close to us that if we had our arms extended out the windows on either side, we could have touched them, In the next instant we realized we had just driven between two moose that were making their way across this major highway. The weather causing limited visibility along with the dark body images made it impossible to see them in any kind of distance. Knowing definitely that these images were moose with that distinguishable hump caught our eye in the short seconds that totaled the timing of the event.

The reality of what had just happened shook us to the core. We asked each other, "Did you see what I just saw?" Exchanging our thoughts, knowing we both had seen the same thing, assured us our imaginations were not running wild.

Knowing the speed in which we were traveling and the size of these animals, survival in this kind of accident would be impossible. My uncle's truck would have been a total loss along with a fatality on our part. We continued to travel in a state of shock, trying to internalize what we had just instantly experienced. Shaking all the way in our return to my mother's, we vowed to each other to tell no one, especially our uncle that we had almost destroyed his truck.

I have to question the timing of my reading of that one particular verse in her Bible only a couple days prior to our near fatal accident. Was this a God whisper which I had not recognized at the time? It amazes me that the only verse which my eyes so casually and unintentionally read related so emphatically to our lives within that short time frame. It comes as a revelation to me that God wants us to be aware that He does intervene in our lives when He chooses, sparing our lives for a Divine purpose. If I had not seen that verse prior to the potential accident, the impact of this truth perhaps would have been diminished. My time, nor my daughter's was not up yet. Sometimes God does more than whisper when delivering His messages to us. But also our lives can be changed in an instant.

When I go back in my memory reflecting on major reflective moments, life-threatening events and life's turning points, God's performing miracles come to mind. I bow my spirit in thanksgiving for the miracles of preservation God has granted me.

God has proven the truth of His promises and whispers can be loaded with direction setting moments.

"Ask and you will receive, seek and you will find, knock and it will be opened to you." Matthew 7:7

Silent Tears

On Hallowed Ground

The yard is quiet now
And the dust is settled.
A doe crosses the lawn gracefully,
Leaping the fence to the other side.

The sun is high
And the grass is tall.
Much taller
Than ever before.

The doors are quiet,
No squeaking of hinges.
The gates stand open,
No one to keep in.

But the stream keeps flowing,
And the spring keeps bubbling.
The grass grows greener,
For all who have gone before.

I have come here many times
And I will come a thousand more.
Because I see not quiet fields and empty pens
But images of happy days.

I see a girl on a horse,
And a boy hugging a calf.
I see children running to hug grandparents,
And tears each time they part.

Selma J. Stroebel

I see goats and chickens,
Cows and sheep,
Dogs and kittens,
And rabbits.

I see cousins at play,
Catching up for time apart.
I see singing by the piano,
Kazoos and a drum.

I see a garden of strawberries
And lots of peas too.
Flowers, onions, garlic,
And.......what's that goat doing in the garden?

I see Grandpa up early,
Driving cows to pasture,
And Grandma's out helping a new lamb.
We follow them both on the chores they must do.

Now a ride on Snooky and Judy
To go out to the field,
To follow the cows
And watch the sun set.

I see tall skinny pines
And a prairie rose over there,
If you go out in the woods,
TALK LOUD, and watch for a bear.

Silent Tears

We can't see the coyotes,
But we know they are near.
Their destruction and howling
Keep us in fear.

Picnics and laughing,
A little play by the river.
Songs and stories
Told to the young by the old.

And so it goes on
Scene after scene.
Though quieter now,
Yet vivid and keen.

Cry not for this past,
Though it's too good to lose.
For there we were loved,
In those cherished rooms.

And there we will stay,
In our memories, our minds,
In our hearts, in our words,
In what is ahead and what was behind.

Cry instead for a place
Where no one has grown.
Where love has not been sought
And loves not been sown.

Selma J. Stroebel

Cry instead for a place
Where an egg's not been found.
Where birth and death
Have no hallowed ground.

Author: (daughter) Karen Stroebel Taylor

Made in the USA
Charleston, SC
19 October 2016